Child Protection Work

Beyond the Rhetoric

Helen Buckley

Jessica Kingsley Publishers
London and Philadelphia

First published in the United Kingdom in 2003
by Jessica Kingsley Publishers Ltd
116 Pentonville Road
London N1 9JB, England
and
325 Chestnut Street
Philadelphia, PA 19106, USA

www.jkp.com

Copyright ©2003 Helen Buckley

Library of Congress Cataloging in Publication Data

Buckley, Helen, 1951-
    Child protection work : beyond rhetoric / Helen Buckley.
        p. Cm.
    Includes bibliographical references and index.
    ISBN 1-84310-075-4 (pbk. : alk. Paper)
    1. Child welfare--Ireland. 2. Child abuse--Ireland. 3. Children--Legal status, laws, etc.--Ireland. 4. Social work with children--Ireland. I. Title.

HV757.A6 B835 2003
362.7'09417--dc21

2002034078

British Library Cataloguing in Publication Data
A CIP catalogue record for this book is available from the British Library

ISBN 1 84310 075 4

Printed and Bound in Great Britain by
Athenaeum Press, Gateshead, Tyne and Wear

Contents

This book is dedicated to the memory of my parents,

Jack and Elizabeth Buckley

Acknowledgements

This book is based on a study carried out for a postgraduate degree at the National University of Ireland, Cork. Primarily, I have to acknowledge the inspiration, expert advice and consistent guidance given by my academic supervisor, Professor Harry Ferguson, who never faltered in his generous support of this project.

I also thank my former line managers and senior management in the organisation in which the study was based, for their substantial contribution towards my academic fees and the extraordinary level of co-operation they granted me. My social work colleagues could not have been more helpful and never complained about my dogged and, I am sure, irritating pursuit of them with a tape recorder for the 12 months that I was conducting fieldwork. Their enthusiasm and interest in the research was an enormous incentive for me to carry on and though it is some time now since we worked together, their different contributions to this study have immortalised each of them for me and I remember them with great affection. Colleagues in different disciplines and agencies involved in child protection and welfare work were equally facilitative and I am very grateful to them all for their time. I greatly appreciated the willingness and openness of the parents who agreed to be interviewed by me and I hope that the finished product does justice to the wealth of data they provided.

My colleagues in the Department of Social Studies, Trinity College Dublin were an unfailing source of support and wisdom during the long and uncertain period of writing up the research. More recently, John Pinkerton and Caroline Skehill, both of Queen's University, Belfast, gave me excellent advice on the drafting of this book. One of the less glamorous tasks involved in publication is proof-reading, and I am particularly grateful to Sadhbh Whelan for her willing assistance in this.

My family accepted my sudden flight into academia with great fortitude. My mother, Elizabeth Buckley, was always proud of anything I did and I am sad that she did not live to see this book published. My sister, Mary Buckley encouraged me all the way as well as giving me considerable practical assistance. My partner, Terry Odlum, sustained me over the years with his patience and generosity, his belief in my ability to complete the work and his constant help and advice. Finally, my son Shane T. Odlum had to live with this project from an early age but made sure, with his wit and his sense of humour, that I never took myself too seriously.

It only remains to be said that ultimate responsibility for the content of the book rests with me.

Chapter One

Child Protection
The Social Regulation of Parenting

Introduction

This book is based on an empirical study of child protection practice in a statutory setting that was carried out between 1992 and 1997 in the Republic of Ireland, during the early stages of unprecedented development in the Irish child welfare system. Over the previous two decades, the terms 'child abuse' and 'child protection' had gained increasing currency, reinforced from time to time by high profile events that had gradually linked the problem to wider social concerns. Perceived deterioration in family values, failing trust in state and ecclesiastical institutions and previously 'hidden' issues such as domestic violence and institutional abuse had become the subject of frequent discussion and debate. As with other social problems, heightened awareness and anxiety about child maltreatment had provided a channel through which various causes were advanced. Interest and pressure groups, along with voluntary and statutory services, all underwent major expansions in terms of both volume and public profile. In addition to new legislation in the form of the Child Care Act 1991,[1] which achieved full implementation in 1996, and a new Children Bill which was later revised and finally enacted as the Children Act 2001,[2] the statutory child care services in Ireland and elsewhere had been progressively subjected to a type of streamlining by the introduction of protocols and procedures (Department of Health 1987, 1995; Department of Education 1991; Irish Catholic Bishops 1996). For the first time, child abuse had become a political issue and serious investment was committed to the development of the child welfare system, reflecting recognition of existing deficiencies in service provision. Debates about the desirability or otherwise of mandatory reporting regularly arose in response to high profile cases where inter-professional communication was seen to be faulty (Department of Health 1996, 1997) and a commitment was made to revise the existing national child protection guidelines in line with new legislation and structural arrangements, culminating in the publication of *Children First: National Guidelines for the Protection and Welfare of Children* in 1999.

Inevitably, anxiety about the problem of child abuse as well as increased investment in the child welfare system in Ireland, the UK and elsewhere has placed services under greater public scrutiny. Paradoxically, political reassurances that scandalous events would never be allowed to happen again carry with them a suggestion of unlimited and unrealistic potential for dealing with and preventing child abuse, putting the system under further pressure. The natural corollary to this is that failure to reach this goal renders the practitioners charged with statutory obligations seriously culpable. It could be argued that the current 'version' of child protection rests on the assumption that child abuse is an objectively identifiable and preventable problem, once sufficient knowledge about its occurrence is disseminated and skills to deal with it have been transmitted. Yet, at the time of writing this book, two fatal child abuse cases in the UK were making the news headlines and the first public child abuse inquiry in the UK for over a decade, on the events surrounding the death of Victoria Climbié, was in process. These facts serve as depressing reminders of the complexity and fallibility of child protection work. It seems that certain crucial elements of professional practice are subject to influences that will continue to transcend legal, policy and service developments whatever infrastructure is in place. Child protection work, as this book will argue, is not amenable to technical rationality but requires constant critical evaluation and reflection as well as an appreciation of its fluid and dynamic nature.

The purpose of this book is not to explore the nature of child abuse per se, nor the factors that cause it or are associated with its occurrence. Its principal focus is on the professional practices of social workers and others employed in the child protection network. It is the nature of this work that the book seeks to explore, through an empirical study that aims to make visible the practices of which it is comprised, in their 'real-life' environments. A number of existing studies address the issues of the prevalence and incidence of child abuse but, as Parton (1996a) argues, there remains a gap in the literature concerning the actual 'work' of child protection at all stages, particularly in relation to the sense-making, selection, categorisation and decision-making processes applied by front-line workers. The Department of Health research programme conducted in the UK in the early 1990s went some way towards examining the child protection system, but more in-depth exposition and analysis of the day-to-day activities of practitioners is required. In seeking to address the gap, this book attempts to challenge the assumptions inherent in the 'official' version of child protection by going beyond descriptions of child protection practice in the idealised sense, to show what workers actually 'do'. It highlights three important issues. First, it illustrates the complex nature of child protection work and the many interacting elements that determine assessment and decision-making. Second, it demonstrates the way in which lack of understanding of and reflectiveness on the nature of these processes can distort the purpose and function of professional practice. Third, it proposes that the operational framework adopted by the statutory agencies increasingly stultifies the values and ideologies that were intended to drive the system.

The research upon which this book is based was initially founded on a number of propositions, emanating from the existing knowledge base on child protection. The way in which the evolution of 'child abuse' has been examined in the literature has provided a useful template that helped to determine the initial design and the data gathering, and later, the analysis and presentation of the material. Within this theoretical framework, the conceptualisation of 'child abuse' as an objective reality is acknowledged to be problematic, constructed as it is through cultural, political, professional and ideological perspectives. The historical accounts offered by Donzelot (1980), Parton (1985), Gordon (1989) and Ferguson (1990, 1994), amongst others, have highlighted the way that concerns that we now know as 'child abuse' were defined very much in contemporary terms that shaped them according to political and popular ideologies and provided a useful backdrop for an examination of the current child protection system. Dingwall, Eekelaar and Murray's (1983) conceptualisation of the way that child abuse is defined as 'the practical reflection of a liberal philosophy', with its component theories of 'the rule of optimism', 'the liberal compromise', and the 'division of regulatory labour' enabled the study to make visible the bureaucratic and occupational frames through which reported concerns about children were constructed by child protection workers. It also guided an exploration of the attitudes and willingness of practitioners with regard to intrusions into family privacy. To further explicate the meanings which were applied to the information gathered by practitioners, Thorpe's (1994) representation of child protection work as an activity determined by 'situated moral reasoning' stimulated the consideration of a number of important themes, particularly the criteria used to measure 'harm' and 'risk' and the type of standards employed to make judgements of seriousness. Christine Parton's (1990) theoretical analysis of the feminist perspective, together with Milner's (1993) observations on the gendered nature of child protection work, have enabled this study to adopt a more gender-sensitive orientation.

Even with the adoption of these theories, the dynamic nature of child protection work still needed to be explained. Reder, Duncan and Gray's (1993) analysis of the interactional processes that occur between the various elements in the system (the professionals, the different agencies, and the families) offered a very useful approach through which relationships, 'stuckness', hostilities, defensive behaviours, and consequent 'failures' could be made explicit. Consideration of other relational difficulties, as identified by Hallett and Birchall (1992), has highlighted a range of rationalisations that could be applied to inter-agency and inter-professional issues. Closer to home, Pithouse's (1987, p.24) explication of the localised practice norms employed by social workers to resolve the 'uncertain and contested endeavours' which their work involved, served to highlight an important area. It emphasised the importance of paying attention to the shared collegial assumptions, rituals and compromises that derive from their occupational culture.

At the time that the fieldwork for this study was being carried out, a body of research on child protection interventions was beginning to emerge in the UK (Thoburn 1993; Farmer 1993; Gibbons and Bell 1994). An identifiable trend in these studies suggested a slippage between, on the one hand, the objective of the child protection system to protect children and promote their well-being and, on the other hand, the way in which it was being perceived both by practitioners whose role it was to operate it and by the families who were subject to investigation. Despite certain administrative and structural differences between the British and Irish systems, these works contributed usefully to the theoretical propositions employed at the outset of this research. A number of the studies, which were published individually in 1995 (Thoburn *et al.* 1995; Farmer and Owen 1995; Gibbons, Conroy and Bell 1995; Cleaver and Freeman 1995) and summarised in a document called *Messages from Research* (Department of Health [UK]) in 1995, later provided useful guidance for the analysis of the findings.

Since the fieldwork for this research was conducted, a number of other important issues have been highlighted in the literature. In the UK, *Messages from Research* has been critiqued on several levels. The methodological approach adopted by some of the studies was considered too narrow (Parton 1996a, Trinder 1996). Additionally, its recommendation for a re-structuring of the current system in the UK in order to achieve a 're-focusing' from *investigation* to assessment of '*need*' was considered misleading. Parton (1997) and Parton, Thorpe and Wattam (1997) offered analyses of this proposed change in approach, highlighting the way that it ignores wider contextual and social issues which have contributed to the construction of the current child protection discourse, and places social workers in an untenable situation where they are expected to resolve problems over which they have little control. Parton (1997) argued that, while there is plenty of evidence to confirm that poverty and marginalisation are strongly represented in families who are subject to child protection interventions (Farmer and Owen 1995; Gibbons *et al.* 1995; Thorpe 1994), the research overview made no link between 'need' and such factors as patriarchy, social class and social fragmentation, but appeared to assume that all that was required was a 'change in front-line professionals' attitudes, re-labelling procedures and minor modifications to operational perspectives and practices' (p.11). He cited other evidence to indicate that the threatening effect of child abuse inquiries, which were so influential in shaping the work of child protection, is still present. Within this context, he argued, the concept of 'integration' of child protection and family support services mooted in *Messages From Research* is an over-simplified one.

This argument was taken further by Parton *et al.* (1997), who offered a deconstruction of the 'work' of child protection, showing the methods by which child abuse becomes organisationally defined and processed. They argued that workers used *professional, organisational,* and *culturally bound* methods of processing information, applying what they termed 'situated moral reasoning' to each and every situation of potential child maltreatment that was presented to them. Such reasoning, they claimed, was comprised largely of opinions about children's behaviours interpreted through referrers and parents, and judgements about mother's parenting and protective capacities; a practice which, they asserted, conforms more to a notion of risk *insurance* rather than risk *assessment.* 'Moral statements', according to Parton *et al.* underpin the construction of maternal identity that is so integral to risk assessment. Their central argument was that interventions tend to be centred on measurement of potential harm; the orientation is forensic rather than preventative, and once the 'danger' abates, the child protection workers withdraw. Parton *et al.* contended that a transfer of resources from child protection to family support would require some radical re-construction of the discourse towards a greater tolerance of uncertainty and a consideration of the structural causes of child maltreatment. The publication, since *Messages from Research,* of the *Framework for the Assessment of Children in Need and their Families,* makes a brave attempt at initiating this shift, but its capacity to achieve it has yet to be judged.

The literature on child protection, rather than providing a rock-solid body of proven theory about the rights and wrongs of different approaches, demonstrates more than anything the constantly moving parameters around the subject. It belies any notion that child abuse is an objectively identifiable or predictable condition, or that the means to address it are either easily applied, or unfailingly effective. On the contrary, the available research evidence offers a picture of a phenomenon that is socially constructed, difficult to reify, and inextricably linked with the prevailing ideological and political climate in a particular society at a given time. It also illustrates the critical balance between intervention and potential social costs, in terms of the negative impact that investigation can have on those implicated in reports. In summary, the literature provided a firm grasp of the theoretical issues that I needed to take further in the research, and affirmed my objective, namely, to make explicit the sense-making activities of practitioners through an empirical study, and thereby to explain the way that child protection 'works'.

While the study upon which this book is based has been principally underpinned by theoretical concepts, it has also been strongly influenced by my 20 years' experience as a practising social worker, during which time I became increasingly aware of a divergence between the way in which the work was actually experienced by practitioners and service users and the perceptions which were held by other stakeholders such as politicians, senior managers in child protection agencies and the general public. The inseparability of the notion of 'child abuse' from its social context, and the way in which it is constructed historically as a problem have been the subject of much academic study (Dingwall *et al.* 1983; Parton 1985; Gordon 1989; Ferguson 1990). In a similar sociological vein, this book proposes that legislation, policies and procedures which are geared towards addressing the problem of child abuse contain inherent assumptions of feasibility and universal applicability which are not necessarily appropriate. It argues that far from being a straightforward and easily defined operation, the work of child protection is replete with contradictions, ideological dilemmas and dynamic elements all of which must be considered and addressed by practitioners and managers if their work is to be effective.

The research

During the early 1990s when the fieldwork for this study was conducted, the development of the Irish child welfare system was at an early stage and its impact was scarcely visible. Ironically, one of the positive effects of the relative stagnation in services had been a high level of stability within child protection and welfare agencies. The dearth of opportunity for change or career advancement meant that practitioners stayed in their posts for prolonged periods, gaining not only experience but in-depth knowledge of the communities they worked in and familiarity with the range of professionals and agencies whose territory they shared. For research purposes, this type of semi-permanence has enormous advantages as it not only facilitates reliability and validity by ensuring a stable body of research participants, but it permits qualitative exploration of the type of well-established practices and norms that evolve within organisations over time. It can be argued, therefore, that despite the many recent and positive developments in the scale of the child protection system in Ireland and elsewhere (see Buckley 2002), many of the issues raised in this book remain as pertinent as they were ten years ago.

The study was based on an in-depth examination of the total number of referrals[3] (72) made to a local authority (known in Ireland as a health board) social work team over the first six months of that period which were designated to the category of 'child abuse/neglect'. Those referrals which were allocated for further work, becoming 'cases', were followed up over a further six months. The research process concentrated initially on the points at which child abuse allegations were reported to the agency, and the trajectory between reporting and the activation of the child protection system where crucial discriminations were made and constructions of 'seriousness' were worked out. Individual interviews were conducted with the social workers who had received the initial reports as soon as possible after the referrals were made. The interviews at this point were open-ended, but focused on a particular set of trigger questions and themes that ensured the study aims were met.

It was the custom in the area where the research was conducted for all referrals to the social work department to be discussed at a weekly 'intake' meeting where decisions were made about further action. The parts of the meeting where child abuse referrals were discussed were taped and provided a rich source of data. They also had the advantage of providing a triangulating device that compensated for certain problems that can occur in interviewing, such as bias or poor recall. In all, 26 intake meetings were observed for the purposes of this research.

As the child abuse reports were processed and filtered, different degrees of intervention and aspects of the child protection machinery were operated, including the use of case conferences (now called child protection conferences). Fourteen of these meetings were observed and recorded for research purposes and the majority of participants were interviewed within the following ten days.

A certain number of child abuse allegations survived the initial filtering processes to become 'cases' and the remainder of the fieldwork period concentrated on these for a further six months, making a total fieldwork period of 12 months. Fourteen of the original seventy-two referrals became cases that were allocated to health board social workers on the area team, and three more were allocated to voluntary agencies. The allocated workers were interviewed at intervals of approximately two months throughout the fieldwork period. In all, 237 interviews were conducted over the entire research period. A fourth source of data comprised of tape-recordings of five meetings which were held during the fieldwork period which were not in either the intake or case conference category, but were set up with the specific purpose of discussing issues about responding to reports of child abuse, and the issue of notifying suspected child abuse to the police (known in Ireland as the Gardaí or An Garda Síochána).

The child protection system

The personal social services, of which child protection work is one dimension, are managed in Ireland on a regional basis. Under the system operating at the time the fieldwork for this study was undertaken, eight local authorities, known as health boards, administered three programmes: the Special Hospital Programme, the General Hospital Programme and the Community Care Programme. The child protection system operated within the Community Care Programme and each region was divided into community care areas. A re-structuring of the health and social services is currently under way following a strategy launched in 1994 and known as *Shaping a Healthier Future* (Department of Health 1994). In addition, the child protection service has developed significantly since the fieldwork for this study was conducted, with an expansion of the numbers of social workers employed, the appointment of child care workers and family support workers and a new line management structure including the appointment of child care managers (see Buckley 2002). In that regard, this research may appear already rather dated. However, the principal themes, particularly the practice issues, which emerge from this study bear little relationship to the structures that existed either then or currently and transcend many of the policy developments that have taken place.

Ballyowen

The area in which this research was based, here called 'Ballyowen', was one sector of a local authority catchment area. It had a population at the time of the fieldwork of roughly 120,000 persons of whom about one fifth were under 18 years of age. Available demographic information could be taken to infer that Ballyowen was at the time a marginally less deprived area than some other sectors in the region. For example, it had lower numbers of unemployed persons, lower numbers of non-marital and teenage pregnancies, lower numbers of persons covered by free (means tested) medical services and the third lowest number of child abuse referrals in the region. It could, therefore, be reasonably assumed that stress upon families was of a slightly lesser degree than might be found in the more disadvantaged parts of the area.

The social work team[4]

At the time the fieldwork for this study was carried out, the social work team covering this population of 120,000 persons consisted of 12 social workers, one of whom joined the team very early in the study period filling a newly established post, and a social work manager. The team included four 'specialists': a community worker, a social worker specialising in fostering and two social workers attached to the adult mental health service for the area. The other eight social workers each carried an average of 30 to 35 child care cases, including medium to long-term child protection work with families where children were deemed 'at risk'; recruitment and support of foster parents; direct work with children in foster and residential care and their birth parents and a small amount of 'tracing' with adults who had been adopted as children. With the exception of the community worker and the mental health social workers, all the social workers regularly covered 'duty', that is, they were available for specified periods when the office was open to members of the public and other professionals to refer themselves or others for a social work service.

When the social work manager was absent, his place was taken by one of the social work team in an acting capacity. In Ballyowen at the time of the study, ten of the twelve social workers had over ten years experience in social work, six of those having practised for over 15 years. Most of the team had spent more than half their social work careers working in Ballyowen, an unusual phenomenon in this profession, where there tends to be a fairly regular turnover of staff. The majority of team members were in their early to mid forties, and the youngest was 33. While several of them had practised social work outside Ireland, mainly in the UK, all the team but one were of Irish nationality, and one was English. Seven of the social workers had completed their professional training in the UK and eleven of them had university degrees prior to gaining their social work qualification. The female/male ratio was nine to four, reflecting a higher percentage of males than the average national norm in the profession at the time of four females to one male (Doherty 1996). In summary, this was a group of social workers with a wealth of practice experience, used to working together as a team and very familiar with the geographical area in which they were based.

Under the system operating at the time of the study, the social work manager was accountable to a senior manager known as the Director of Community Care.[5] According to the child abuse guidelines operating at the time (Department of Health 1987), the Director of Community Care, or a senior area medical officer designated by the Director, was deemed responsible for child protection in his or her area. In this study, that duty had been designated to a senior area medical officer, who acted on behalf of the Director. All notifications of child abuse were made to her, and she convened and chaired case conferences. It was also her responsibility to maintain and review the list of cases where child abuse had been confirmed or suspected.

The duty system

The 'intake' social work service in Ballyowen was administered through a 'duty' system, according to which a social worker was available to the public each day between 9am and 5pm. There was an expectation that work requiring urgent action would be completed the same day, even if that meant working late into the evening. There was no local 'out of hours' service. Duty social workers provided a referral and information service to all members of the public who attended, whatever their age or the subject of their query. However, as the study develops, it will be observed that only child care matters were taken up for further work, and allocated as cases.

Unlike some other community care areas, the Ballyowen social workers were not attached to any particular 'patch' or sector, and cases were allocated to them at weekly team meetings. Generally, they volunteered to take on cases. Otherwise the social work manager allocated them according to his perception of the workers' particular abilities or space in their workload. Occasionally, a waiting list operated. More commonly, unallocated cases remained 'open on duty' to be dealt with by different workers as the need arose. Child protection, that is reports of alleged harm to or neglect of children, generally took priority. The willingness of the social workers to take on cases was overtly based on their capacity to take on more work, although as the research findings are developed, motives for making and taking allocations will be shown to be far more convoluted.

In Ballyowen, there were 237 referrals to the duty system during the fieldwork period. The breakdown is illustrated in Table 1.1.

Table 1.1 Referrals to the social work duty system during the first phase of the fieldwork period (1 October 1993 to 31 March 1994)	
Child Abuse/neglect	72
Information	41
Family support	28
Adolescents	13
Financial	10
Homelessness	9
Adoption/tracing	9
Mental health problems	7
Pregnancy counselling	7
Addiction	7
Fostering	5
Requests for care	5
Elderly	4
Physical illness/disability	4
Counselling	2
Other*	14
Total	**237**

mainly concerning issues that did not fit into categories, for example, complaints about neighbours, or enquiries about non-social work related matters

The child abuse/neglect referrals included in Table 1.1 form the basis of this study. The classifications in Table 1.1 were listed in the intake book wherein social workers allocated referrals to the different categories as they saw fit. Essentially, as will become clearer, they made swift but crucial judgements; though these were open to modification at the team meetings, the initial decisions often profoundly affected the course of the referrals.

The processing of referrals

In Ballyowen, referrals were made to the social work team either directly by members of the public, or by professionals who were either reporting their own concerns or those which may have been passed to them by members of the public. If the matter reported appeared to be urgent, for example if it concerned a child who was at immediate or serious risk, it would receive immediate attention. Otherwise, it may have been dealt with in one of the following ways:

1. the duty worker remained responsible for it until it was resolved

2. it was passed on to the duty social worker the following day

3. it was allocated at the team meeting for further investigation or intervention.

At the weekly team meeting, the social work manager recorded the disposal of the referral, that is, if it was closed, transferred or allocated, and to whom. The child abuse guidelines operating at the time (Department of Health 1987) outlined a step by step procedure for responding to suspected child abuse and neglect, and reports of this kind to the duty social worker should have normally followed the suggested course, which was to formally notify the social work manager and Director of Community Care. In practice, this process was subject to many contingencies that will be illuminated in the remaining chapters of this book. However, in theory, there was an accepted routine for the processing of such referrals, which will now be described.

It was normal practice for the duty social worker to endeavour to speak face to face with the person who first voiced the concern about the child or children, particularly if that person was not the actual referrer. It was also policy to initiate the investigation by gathering as much information as possible about the subjects from other professionals likely to have known them, typically the public health nurse[6] or another agency that might have been involved.

Having established the initial concerns, social workers would endeavour to piece together a picture of the situation, sharing information with his or her line managers. Consultations could take place with legal advisors if the child or children's immediate safety appeared to be in jeopardy and, if grounds for legal intervention existed, arrangements could be made for the social worker involved to swear an affidavit in front of a judge in order to obtain an emergency care order. During the field-work period for this study, emergency orders were taken on three children, from two different cases. However, none of the orders were executed during the initial investigation phase.

If physical abuse had been alleged, a medical examination would normally have been deemed necessary, and the child's general practitioner or an area medical officer would have carried this out. Alternatively, a child could be seen at a hospital casualty department. Medical examinations were considered necessary for only two of the children referred during this study, one of whom had allegedly been beaten by his mother and another who had disclosed sexual abuse.

Child sexual abuse allegations in Ballyowen were frequently referred to the child sexual abuse assessment service designated for the area, which operated in a hospital. A written report would be sent to the service, and if it were deemed an appropriate referral by the staff, an appointment for assessment would be offered to the children and carers. Of the children featuring in the study, four were referred for child sexual abuse assessment, from three different cases.

Sixteen case conferences were held to discuss reports that had been made during the first six months of the fieldwork period for this study.

An important element of the initial stage of the child protection process needs to be highlighted at this point. The term 'report' or 'referral' refers to the initial concern or incident that would have ultimately come to the attention, possibly through the medium of other professionals, of the health board social worker on duty. Depending on the seriousness of a concern, it may or may not have been discussed between the social worker and the social work manager. Normally, if a concern appeared to constitute child abuse, a brief, written notification of the allegation would be made to the Director on the same day, using a specific set of forms designed for the purpose. This process was known officially as 'notifying' the Director. It is important to note the distinction between a 'referral' or 'report' and a 'notification'; the significance of the latter will become clearer as the study findings are developed. This process is now explicitly outlined in the most recent child protection guidelines published in Ireland (Department of Health and Children 1999) and is known as the CPNS (Child Protection Notification System). It is similar to the process that was operating in Ballyowen at the time of the study, but includes notification to the police and discussion with a multi-disciplinary group before the process is complete. Essentially, the process of 'notification' could be tentatively compared with the process of registration carried out in the UK child protection system, though its implications and consequences would be different. The main similarity would be that the process of notification was the means by which a report of alleged or actual child abuse entered the 'official' system and would be calculated in annual statistics. It would also come under the scrutiny of management, who would assume overall responsibility for it. At the time the fieldwork for this study was conducted, any child abuse allegation that was not notified would not be counted in the annual returns, nor would it come to the attention of any manager in the health board system above the social work manager. Of the 72 referrals which were classified by the social workers in Ballyowen as 'child abuse/neglect' during the study period, only 17 were 'notified'. The reasons for this stark difference will be discussed in full in Chapter Two.

During the first six-month fieldwork period, 14 (including some, but not all of the 'notified' referrals) of the 72 referrals of suspected child abuse were eventually allocated to social workers on the community care team for ongoing work, and two others were deemed 'open' but were managed by the area child psychiatric service which was delivered by a voluntary agency. One other case was held by the social worker in a voluntary service for children with physical disabilities. This meant that just under 25 per cent of child protection cases remained open beyond investigation, a figure consistent with UK research carried out around the same time (Gibbons *et al.* 1995).

Of the other 165 non-child protection referrals, only ten were allo-cated as cases for ongoing, generally short-term, work. The fostering worker and the mental health social workers picked up four cases between them, connected with their own specialities. Five cases were allocated to a social work student on placement, concerning the areas of housing, custody, mental illness and pregnancy counselling. Only one non-child protection case was allocated apart from those, and was open for only a very short time. This practice affirms current theories which suggest the narrowing of what was originally a generic social work service to one which focuses quite narrowly on child protection (Ferguson 1994, 1996; Parton 1991, 1996; Thorpe 1994; Buckley, Skehill and O'Sullivan 1997).

Conclusion

What has been described above is the recommended practice or official rhetoric for the processing of child abuse referrals. In reality, however, timing of the individual stages differs considerably according to the vari-ables involved in each situation, particularly with regard to the perceived risk or danger to the children involved. But more significantly for this study, each step in the process is influenced by a number of events that have less to do with policy and procedure than with implicit team and agency norms which are largely unacknowledged. These contingencies, which rarely feature in any social work or child protection texts and never in any policy document, will be illuminated and analysed during the course of the study. The following chapter will start to make this process explicit, beginning with a discussion of the initial agency response to reports that were considered to refer to abuse or neglect of children.

Endnotes

1   The Child Care Act 1991 replaces the Children Act 1908 in respect of children who are not receiving adequate care and protection. It is principally concerned with promotion of welfare, with emphasis on the child's right to be brought up in his or her family, and it provides for a range of care orders to be used as a last resort.

2   The Children Act 2001 replaces the Children Act 1908 in respect of juvenile justice and provides for a number of legal measures including special care orders for non offending children in need of secure care. Like the

Child Care Act 1991, its main thrust is proactive; it emphasises parental rights and responsibilities and advocates diversion and restorative justice with detention to be used only when other options have failed.

3   A 'referral' essentially means a report, or a contact which is made by either a member of the public or a professional, seeking a service.

4   Throughout the book, I refer to social workers on the Health Board community care team as 'social workers', 'duty social workers' (where appropriate) or 'Health Board social workers'. Some research participants refer to them as 'community care' social workers. Essentially, these terms are interchangeable, and where I have interviewed social workers from an agency other than the Health Board, I have specifically identified that fact.

5   This post has now been abolished and the management of child abuse reports is currently the responsibility of the Child Care Manager.

6   In Ireland, the public health nurse has a similar child protection and welfare brief to that of the health visitor in the UK; the main difference between the two professions is the fact that public health nurses in Ireland also have a brief for curative nursing.

Chapter Two

'Constructing' Child Abuse

Identifying child abuse and neglect

The degree to which definition and acknowledgement of different forms of child maltreatment depend for their existence on a particular set of social circumstances has been debated in the literature over several decades. In the late 1970s Giovannoni and Becerra (1979) illustrated how, in their Californian study, professional perceptions differed from those of lay persons and how, even amongst the former, thresholds of seriousness could be perceived differently. Dingwall *et al.* (1983) in an English study carried out around the same period, suggested that the moral evaluation of parenting is only possible when the behaviour of adults towards children is placed in a social context. More recent research in the UK has argued that child maltreatment is a socially constructed phenomenon (Gibbons *et al.* 1995; Department of Health [UK] 1995; Parton *et al.* 1997). As the introductory chapter has shown, a certain fusion of events can combine at any time to either raise or lower the possibilities for the construction of certain types of actions within the framework of abuse, and consideration of some contemporary events in Ireland offers an illustration of how such a process was effected in this country.

At the time this study was undertaken, the *Report of the Kilkenny Incest Investigation* (Department of Health 1993) had recently been published in Ireland. The increase in referrals of suspected child abuse to the statutory services following the report's publication bore testimony to the fact that the recognition of child abuse, child sexual abuse in particular, had become culturally feasible in Ireland. According to Department of Health statistics, the rate of child abuse reporting to the health boards rose by 25 per cent nationally from 4110 to 5152 between 1993 and 1994 (Department of Health 1996b). The increase in Ballyowen during the same period was 10 per cent. The figures have continued to rise, the most recent statistics available indicating a figure of 10,031 for 1999 (Department of Health and Children 2000). Seen in this context, it could be claimed this research study was situated at a fairly active stage in the transition from a comparative complacence to a 'radicalisation' (Ferguson 1996, p.26) of political and public concern about child maltreatment. Essentially, however, it is unlikely that the process of deciding on the veracity or otherwise of reported child protection concerns has fundamentally altered. This chapter describes how it was mediated at agency level and explicates the various terms in which categorisations were organisationally defined.

Child abuse referrals

Social workers in child protection provide a reactive rather than a proactive service, rarely encountering situations of abuse themselves. Rather, they receive and process information. The informants are either professionals or lay people, and passing reports to the official system is known in the professional language as 'making a referral', which may or may not evolve into a 'case'. Pithouse (1987, p.11) described a social work 'case' as the 'basic organisational unit that is intended to document a specific service to a specific consumer'. Reports of child abuse did not become 'cases' in this study until they had been 'allocated' to a specific worker to undertake a designated piece of work. Consequently, the organisational unit that was the focus of the first part of the study is the 'referral'.

Child abuse referrals to the Ballyowen social work team were made through a variety of channels, typically by telephone or a personal call to the office. Some were made directly to the social workers, others through different personnel, but they inevitably found their way to the duty social worker's desk. It is important to note that when referrals were made, they were not necessarily presented in terms of child 'abuse'. Rather, a message or account would be given of a situation that gave rise to some concern about a particular child or children. In other words, the framing of certain circumstances and events as 'child abuse' was merely *initiated* by professionals and lay people in the community who wished to bring their concerns to the attention of the statutory agency whose responsibility it was to deal with such matters. The act of classifying the concern as 'child abuse' or giving it another designation was normally carried out by the duty social worker, who had the primary task of deciding what behaviour or consequences would constitute 'abuse' and what would not. The role played by the duty workers was essentially that of official gatekeepers who would determine whether referrals ever had the chance to become cases.

By categorising and recording a referral as 'child abuse/neglect' in the intake system, a social worker initiated a process that potentially placed a report on the official treadmill of investigation. As the previous chapter has indicated, taking the further step of 'notifying' the concern to the Director not only signalled the perceived seriousness of the matter under consideration, but generated a chain of activity which made practitioners accountable to a higher layer of management than would be the case otherwise. These two important but not necessarily sequential acts, the initial categorising of a referral as alleged 'child abuse', and the notification of the concern were crucial in determining the level of investigative response to be made, and warrant serious examination in this chapter. At this point, however, some consideration of the nature and path of referrals will provide further contextual information through which the aforementioned processes can be better understood.

During the first six-month phase of the study period, a total of 72 'child abuse/neglect' reports were entered into the intake system by the Ballyowen social work team. These comprised 68 new referrals and four re-referrals during the same period. In other words, in four cases, the original concerns having been resolved and the matter having been closed, the families were referred for a second time. On looking at the records, it was not always possible to ascertain how many children were in each family, as some initial reports were not processed to the point of gathering such detail. However, it appeared from the available information that there were 155 children in the reported families, the 'child abuse' concerns referring to a total of 144 children.

While 17 of the reports alluded to more than one type of concern, it was normal for a particular type of 'abuse' to dominate the suspicions of either the referrers or the social workers who classified the referrals, as shown in Table 2.1. The generic category of 'child abuse/neglect' was the only one used in the intake system at the time, so the specific classification of physical, sexual and emotional abuse and neglect are based on my interpretation of the social work interviews and intake meeting discussions, according to how the social workers themselves appeared to categorise the principal concern.

Table 2.1 Child abuse referrals	
Physical abuse	13
Child sexual abuse	21
Emotional abuse	4
Neglect	34
Total	**72**

Most child abuse statistics will illustrate the origin of referrals in terms of the person or agency that brings the information about a child protection concern to the attention of a statutory body. However, they will not necessarily explicate the referral path, i.e. the number and the designation of persons who are involved in communicating the information from its original source. As Table 2.2 will illustrate, 39 referrals were made directly to the Health Board[1] during the study period by professionals and members of the public who *first* witnessed the abusive incident, or experienced the concern about the child or children involved. Within this category, police and medical social workers made four referrals each, teachers made three, the child psychiatric services referred three, Health Board social workers from other areas referred two, and there was one direct referral each from a school attendance officer, a local authority housing welfare officer and a general practitioner. The remainder came from members of the public, one who was himself a victim of the abuse he was reporting. Three other referrers were parents, two were otherwise related, the rest were friends or neighbours and one was anonymous.

Table 2.2 Direct Referrals	
Police	4
Medical social workers	4
Teachers	3
Child psychiatric service	3
Other Health Board social workers	2
School attendance officer	1
Housing welfare officer	1
General practitioner	1
Parents	3
Other relatives	2
Victim himself	1
Neighbours/acquaintance/anonymous	14
Total	**39**

In contrast, and as Table 2.3 will show, just under half of the reports came second-hand, or indirectly, to the Health Board and were made by members of the public who chose to contact non-social work professionals rather than making a direct referral to the social work team, or the Director of Community Care/Area Medical Officer. The professionals whom they contacted, in turn, passed the concerns to the social work service. In almost all cases, the duty social worker would endeavour to speak to the person who first identified the risk or harm, though this was not always possible, and as the later part of this chapter will explain, inability to talk to the first person was construed by the social workers as a barrier to investigation. It could be speculated that members of the public chose to make their refer-rals indirectly because they were unaware of the 'correct' procedure, or perhaps because they simply chose a more convenient route. Equally, they could have deliberately avoided contact with social workers, believing that this would obviate a 'heavy' response. Whatever the reason, it became clear the more links that existed in the referral chain, the more possibilities there were for flawed communication to ensue.

Table 2.3 Indirect referrals	
Public health nurses	6
Police	4
General practitioners	4
Medical social workers	3
Teachers	3
Vincent de Paul	2
Parish priest	2
Community welfare officer	3
Child sexual abuse assessment unit	1
Voluntary agency for homelessness	1
Psychologist	1
Landlord	1
Members of the public	2
Total	**33**

The original sources of the indirect referrals were all either neighbours, relatives or members of the public, except for one person, described as a 'relationships' counsellor who made a referral through a school where she was conducting a seminar. Two anonymous callers, who reported their concerns to public health nurses, described themselves as 'neighbours'.

On examination of the above tables, and when the figures are adjusted to allow for the indirect path of some referrals, it can be concluded that 72 per cent of concerns about harm or risk to children, later defined as suspected child abuse, came originally from relatives and members of the public. The other 28 per cent originated from professional sources. This concurs with a later Irish study by Ferguson and O'Reilly (2001), which found that only 36 per cent of child protection referrals were 'authentically' brought to light by professionals. This finding signals the growing awareness of the concept of child abuse by the general public as well as the significant role played by them in the communication of information.

'Pre-screening' of child abuse allegations

Under Section 8 of the Child Care Act 1991, health boards are obliged to produce annual reviews of the adequacy of child care and family support services. These reports normally include statistics comprised of the total number of child abuse reports made to the health boards in any one year, including the number of those reports which were 'confirmed', which is usually under half of the initial referrals. The information from which these statistics are constructed consists of the total numbers of *notified* cases, that is, those that had followed the formal notification route[2] earlier described, into the child protection system. It will be shown here that not all child abuse allegations, or referrals which were initially allocated to the 'child abuse/neglect' category, are necessarily put through this process; many are screened out at an early stage and therefore do not feature in the official figures.

During the first six months of the study period, although 144 children were the subjects of 'child abuse' referrals, insofar as they were designated to that category on initial intake, the reports on only 33[3] of those referred were formally notified. As a result, it can be seen that official statistics represented only a fraction of the 'child abuse/neglect' referrals made to the social work department. What annual returns universally *fail* to signify is the amount of 'pre-screening' that takes place which keeps many reports out of the system, a consequence of which is that official statistics may in fact seriously misrepresent the type of child protection activity that takes place.

In the UK study by Gibbons *et al.* (1995), 25 per cent of child abuse referrals were closed without any investigation. In other UK research, Thoburn, Lewis and Shemmings (1995) show how social workers tend to operate the child abuse guidelines with discretion, sometimes delaying officially prescribed actions until more information can be obtained. This trend was also evident in an Irish study (Buckley *et al.* 1997) where only 60 per cent of cases were processed within the recommended time frame. Various explanations for this type of practice have been offered in the literature, some of which employ organisational theories. Pithouse (1987) has suggested that norms that are unique to the individual agency or team can overrule professional guidelines. He observed that:

> Policies and philosophies that are intended to direct welfare practices are mediated within the work setting and often recede into the wings of an interactive arena, where members assert their own view of appropriate practice. (p.7)

Another 'sifting' priority applied by duty social workers and identified by Wise (1989, p.399), is the need to prevent as many referrals as possible from becoming cases needing allocation, in order to keep the workload manageable. The criteria operated to achieve this, she claims, are based on the 'common-sense practical reasoning of the individual on duty…whose judgement may or may not have utilised the "objective" criteria set by the department'. Using an argument that derives more from sociological concepts, Dingwall *et al.* (1983) have suggested that the selective interpretation of clinical and social criteria provides a screening process that in turn ensures that many cases of child abuse do not get through the system. These interpretations, they suggest, stem from a broad range of social, professional, cultural, and political influences, forming part of the 'liberal compromise' that protects families from interference by the state.

The pre-screening that operated in Ballyowen undoubtedly followed some of the principles asserted in the literature and it was no less complex than the processes suggested above. Clearly, there was a divergence from the official procedures that required all referrals concerning suspected child abuse to be notified. Although categorisation and notification were distinct functions carried out at different times, it is not possible to separate consideration of these concepts in this study, as the latter was very much contingent on the former. Similarly, the possibility of a case being notified appeared to bear more strongly on its potential for being investigated by an interview with the children's parents and later *confirmed* as child abuse, than on its initial 'suspected' status. I have already suggested that the gap between the reported and confirmed cases reflected in child abuse statistics illustrates the level of investigative activity in child protection work. I would also propose that an equally important, though less visible, element of the work lies in the gap between the acts of 'referral' by professionals and members of the public, and 'notification' and investigation carried out by statutory social workers. As the remainder of this chapter shows, pre-screening or 'filtering out' represents a substantial amount of the work of child protection. Given the breadth of interpretations applied with different motives to this activity, it is inevitably fraught with contradictions.

Criteria for categorising a referral as 'child abuse/neglect'

Referrals were categorised as 'child abuse/neglect' in the intake book on the basis of certain factors that emerged in the initial reporting which, whether later endorsed or not, appeared to constitute a working definition of 'abuse' or potential abuse. A typology of these 'risk' factors is shown in Figure 2.1 and represents the constructions through which the category 'child abuse' was *initially* designated by duty social workers who, on receipt of reports, made a quick decision to allocate them to the 'child abuse/neglect' category in the intake book.

The disclosure by children, no matter how young, of sexual approaches on the part of an adult, was always initially categorised as 'abuse'. Likewise, evidence of physical injury, admissions of 'hitting' by parents, or reports by children or other adults of what appeared to be excessive physical punishment, were almost certainly placed in the same category. Physical violence between parents was construed to constitute physical abuse to a child on at least one occasion where an infant got knocked out of his mother's arms when his father hit her. Children under 12 years (approximately) found alone were regarded as 'neglected'. Sexualised behaviour, suspicious injuries, 'rumours' of sexual approaches, suggestions of parental immaturity and reports of inadequate care in terms of clothing, food and shelter were designated to the 'child abuse/neglect' category as well, but as will be shown, were more liable to be discounted after some discussion, and possibly not investigated very assertively. The sort of behaviour that was constructed as 'emotional abuse' tended to be shouting and verbal aggression generally, particularly in a context of alcohol abuse. Again, if the type of social work response that was typically made is used as an indicator, there was no evidence that emotional abuse was prioritised in terms of seriousness.

- Disclosure of sexual abuse by a child
- Disclosure of physical abuse by a child
- Admission of abusive behaviour by parent
- Child's sexualised behaviour (of virtually any degree)
- Previous history of sexual abuse by child's carer or person associated with child
- Reports of suspicious sexual behaviour by an adult towards a child
- Suspicious injury or symptoms of physical abuse
- Excessive discipline, including shouting and hitting
- Lack of proper care, inadequate shelter, clothing or food
- Violence between parents where a child was *actually* injured (rather than considered to be at *risk* of injury)
- Perceived immaturity of female parent
- Dependent children found or suspected of being left unsupervised

---

Figure 2.1 Factors deemed by the social workers to constitute 'risk' to children

Domestic violence as a risk factor did not feature in the general classifications used by social workers to categorise their referrals. It was also clear that domestic violence as a form of child abuse was not part of the definitional framework used at the time this research was carried out, even though it has since been identified as such in a discussion paper on mandatory reporting (Department of Health [Ireland] 1996a) and the more recently published national child protection guidelines (Department of Health and Children [Ireland] 1999) as well as a growing body of literature that emphasises the negative impact on children of living in an environment where domestic violence is recurrent (Mullender 1996; Buckley 2002).

However, the risk factors outlined here mean very little without attention, not only to their content, but to the context in which they arose. In order to illustrate how risk factors are 'weighted', I will describe a typical child abuse case, one of the 72 referrals, which received an immediate and unambiguous response from the social work service. Comparisons between this and other cases may explain some apparent discrepancies in responding to referrals.

The M case

CM was 16 years old when this case came to the attention of the social work team in Ballyowen. She disclosed to a friend that she had been the victim of sexual abuse by her father for several years. C expressed concern that her older and younger siblings were likely to have been abused by their father as well. The friend told her mother, who reported the disclosure, with C's permission, to the duty social worker. The social worker in turn notified the social work manager and the senior area medical officer, and as this referral had been made late in the evening, sent a message via the referrer to tell C she would see her the next day.

The following day, the duty social worker, having taken advice about the legality of speaking to a 16-year-old without her parents' knowledge, spoke at length with C and obtained her permission to discuss the case with her school guidance counsellor. The young girl described how her father had engaged her in oral sex and masturbation and had forced her to look at pornographic material. The social worker then consulted with the senior area medical officer and the social work manager, and an emergency case conference was planned. It had been the practice in Ballyowen, when responding to disclosures of intra-familial sexual abuse, to do as much planning and information gathering as possible prior to confronting the family, even if this meant a few days' delay. The purpose of the case conference was to orchestrate a co-ordinated approach to the family that would minimise the possibility of denial and ultimately provide greater protection for the children.

The case conference was held, chaired by the senior area medical officer and attended by the duty social worker, the social work manager, the school guidance counsellor, and a member of the police. A plan was agreed whereby the social work manager and the duty social worker would visit the family home at a time when they knew that the mother would be on her own, speak to her first about the allegations, and later confront the father, and ask for his co-operation in leaving the family home, pending the investigation. The children were then to be referred, with the parents' agreement, to the child sexual abuse assessment unit, and a further case conference was to be held to discuss future plans.

In its execution, the plan worked like clockwork. The father, after some initial denial, acknowledged that he had abused the children and agreed to leave the family home. The safety of the children was pledged by the mother. The children were referred to the child sexual abuse unit for assessment, and the case was allocated to a social worker.

On reflection, it is relatively easy to see why this referral fitted so well into the framework for 'abuse' that had been constructed and was being operated by the social workers. The nature of the sexual behaviour that was described left little question in anyone's mind about its inappropriateness. There were no doubts about the veracity of the referrer, and the victim had made her disclosure in an articulate and credible fashion. Structures existed for further assessment and treatment. The family were co-operative, including the perpetrator. There was no dispute about who owned responsibility for the case, and the Health Board as the statutory body readily adopted its management role. The police were highly receptive to the conference plan, so a co-ordinated approach was possible.

It can be seen therefore, that a number of elements combined in the M case to obviate the ambivalence and ambiguities frequently associated with responding to child abuse reports. These included the nature of the allegation, and the manner in which it was disclosed. Armed with such evidence, the need to take responsible action eliminated any dilemmas about confronting the parents, and the confrontation was supported and informed by co-operation from other agencies and professionals. The acknowledgement and contrition of the person believed responsible, and the protective attitude of the non-abusing parent facilitated the implementation of interventive strategies. It was undoubtedly with serious cases like this in mind that child abuse guidelines and procedures have been drawn up, and in such instances, they provide useful advice.

However, the elements that unquestioningly facilitated the response, most particularly, the certainty surrounding the referral and definition, are rarely as accessible in the vast majority of referrals made. Yet, as Thorpe (1994), and Parton et al. (1997) suggest, the 'popular' concept of child abuse has been dominated by the relatively low number of serious cases which come to the attention of social services. The impression is given that all incidences of so called 'child abuse' are equally grave, and clearly discernible. As a result, a framework for practice has been created which is based on the sort of confident, uncomplicated and unambiguous approach that is possible in such cases. Yet, this paradigm may not necessarily fit with situations which are less clear, where ambivalence exists, where the credibility or motivation of the referrer may be in doubt and where contextual factors may exist to blur the boundaries between what might be construed as dangerous, harmful, accidental or 'normal' phenomena.

Unlike the M case, many of the child abuse reports on which this research is based left a lot of room for uncertainty about the need for investigation and also allowed space for a number of other obstacles to impede a response. In relation to this study, I have adopted the word 'investigation' to signify a personal interview with the parents or carers of the child who is alleged to be at risk, rather than the inter-agency and inter-professional checks that are normally carried out first. Making personal face-to-face contact with a carer was colloquially known as 'going out' on a case, even though the meeting may actually take place in the office. Because the guidelines dictate that 'child abuse' must be notified and investigated, one of the ways that the workers avoided these actions was to discount, at an early stage, the 'abuse' aspect of the reported concern. I earlier described how the acts of notification and investigation endorsed the 'child abuse' designation. As I will now demonstrate, the opposite could also happen; if the social workers decided against notifying or investigating a report, the perception or suspicion of 'abuse' in the reported concern was automatically discounted.

Weekly team meetings, at which all the referrals for the previous week were discussed in a fairly informal way, provided a forum for refining the original categorisation of cases. In this situation, adherence to the cultural or organisational norms adopted by the team appeared to determine how reports were perceived. Whilst referrals remained allocated to their original classifications, their disposal was very often decided upon as a result of the practitioners' collective views. These frequently acted to modify the meaning or intention of the original report in such a way as to diminish the risk to the children involved. This discounting activity was not simply a result of the convergence of individual opinions, but was shaped by what Pithouse (1987) would term 'collegial' policy. The way that the team of workers in Ballyowen operated supported Pithouse's theory that the colleague group represents 'a structure of meanings and relationships' and a 'reference group', within which social workers tend to make arbitrary use of official rules, believing 'the multiplicity of events and contingencies in cases bears no relation to the abstract generality of broad directives' (p.28).

The M case was responded to quickly because of the undeniable gravity of the sexual abuse committed. Yet, despite the high proportion of referrals concerning sexual activity of some kind, the social workers were aware that defining particular behaviours as 'abusive' often reflected personal values. The threshold at which, for example, sexualised play became abusive appeared very nebulous. This can be illustrated with reference to another allegation, where a general practitioner referred a family to the social work team.

The A case

This report was made 'second-hand' by a public health nurse, but a telephone call by the duty social worker to the mother of the child concerned provided first-hand information. The mother, here called Mrs A reported that some time previously her seven-year-old daughter, B, had had a friend, of the same age, over to her house to play. B later casually mentioned to her mother that she and the friend had been 'playing sex'. When her mother inquired further, B said that her friend had closed the door of the room in which they were playing and started kissing her on the mouth, moving down to her stomach. In response to her mother's query, she said that they had all their clothes on. B allegedly described the experience as 'yucky', and apparently suggested, after some probing by her mother, that her friend had seen people kissing like that on television. Her mother was initially disturbed, but did not pursue the matter, convincing herself that it was innocent child's play. During the following week, B's behaviour became uncharacteristically clingy and she seemed troubled. The public health nurse happened to call to see one of the younger children, and Mrs A mentioned B's behaviour, which she was inclined to connect with other family events that had recently occurred. In response to the nurse's questions, she mentioned the kissing incident. The public health nurse expressed concern about possible child sexual abuse and telephoned the duty health board social worker who in turn contacted Mrs A and spoke to her at length by phone.

When the duty worker who had spoken on the telephone to the mother brought up this matter at the team meeting, the possibility was mooted that the 'other' child (whose name had not been revealed) had been sexually abused and was acting out learned behaviour with B. However, unlike the M case, a straightforward response was not easily formulated. Discussion about the report dominated that week's team meeting for over two hours, with opinions ranging from a recommendation to visit the 'other' child's family and discuss the report with them, to a view that such play was harmless and normal among six- to seven-year-olds. As one worker pointed out:

> You see I don't know what's appropriate behaviour or not, I don't know what sexual play is or not…this business of what's normal and what's not is varying from people to people and their own experience and their own attitudes towards sexuality…

Given this level of uncertainty, the question of whether or not to contact the 'other' family became crucial. It appeared that the act of intervening with the other family would endorse the labelling of the concern as 'suspected sexual abuse', but letting it go was a self-affirming way of closing the referral with no recommendation for further action. The reasons proposed for not contacting the 'other' family were strongly linked to the social workers' uncertainty about the gravity of the incident. This, in turn, was related to their reluctance to impose themselves on families in a way that they perceived as inevitably hostile and negative. As one worker put it:

> Once you make an intervention at all, and we had this before, I think that the impact on people when they hear something nasty about themselves, or something nasty has happened to someone in the family, even if it hasn't huge implications for the family, it has huge knock-on effects...

It was suggested by another worker that the 'other' family had a 'right' to know that the Health Board had information about them, albeit anonymous, and that they could be simply visited in a sort of neutral or non-judgmental way, informed of the report, and asked to respond without the encounter appearing to represent a confrontation or accusation. This suggestion was greeted with scepticism by another social worker who argued:

> Once you go to the family and say this, there's an implication that their child has been sexually abused... I mean what we're in there to find out is did this girl's father abuse her, and if he didn't, then did somebody else, and I mean that's the bottom line...

Ultimately, a follow up visit was made to Mrs A, the mother of the child who spoke about the 'sexual' play, not the child who had initiated it. On the basis of that interview, which elicited little new information about the actual event, the social worker decided to take no further action. Mrs A, according to the worker, 'presented as interested and concerned about her child', and apparently by inference, was protective of her. This seemed to satisfy the duty social worker, though in fact Mrs A's 'protectiveness' of her own child had never been in doubt. During their conversation, the concern associated with the 'other' child seemed to have diminished, though the alleged facts were essentially the same. At the same time, the social worker was conscious that Mrs A did not want her to pursue it:

> She was very worried about what it had led to, the fact that a social worker was actually arriving to her ... she was, I'd say, very sorry that she had gone near anybody, but she was also horrified at the prospect of a social worker arriving at somebody else's house on her say so, as she saw it, because she felt that she would find it dreadful herself if a social worker came to her.

The social worker obviously identified with Mrs A's views on social work contacts. Asked by me if she was satisfied with her decision not to pursue it, she responded:

> I'm as happy as one can be, that I don't know... I have no way of knowing now if that child is being abused or not. I think if I went to visit the family I wouldn't have any way of knowing whether that child is being abused or not either ... I don't know, maybe it's just protecting me ... going to the family with very little substance could have a very devastating effect on them, you know, and I think that ... this is the effect we do have, and could be extremely distressing for them and I didn't feel that it merited that.

The social worker's assessment of the situation was accepted with little discussion and the referral was officially closed, no contact having been made with the 'other' child or her parents. The decision appeared to have been made, not on the basis of an informed assessment of potential or actual sexual abuse of the 'other' child, but as a result of the social worker's 'situated moral reasoning' (Thorpe 1994; Parton *et al.* 1997). The object of adjudication appeared to have been Mrs A's character, including her interest and concern about her own child, which seemed to validate her view that the play was harmless and innocent. It was also strongly influenced by the social worker's dread of 'devastating' the 'other' family by her intervention. She had operated the 'liberal compromise' (Dingwall *et al.* 1983), and the matter was closed without further investigation. Despite the amount of time spent on this referral, it was, for the reasons outlined above, never formally notified, and therefore did not appear in any official statistics. The discretionary culture which operated around the classification of referrals as 'child abuse' or otherwise appeared to be acceptable to the team, as there was no quibble with it, nor any attempt to offer an alternative. It represented 'loyalty towards local views of practice' (Pithouse 1987, p.28), left the way open for a variety of responses, and acted as a sort of safety valve to prevent overloading of the system.

'Filtering' devices used by the social workers

So far, I have illustrated the way that, contrary to the directives of the child abuse guidelines, reported concerns about children did not automatically elicit the type of investigative response that might have been expected. On the contrary, it appeared that a high degree of 'in-house' arbitration took place in relation to each referral, as a result of which only a quarter of the referrals initially categorised as child abuse (18 out of 72) were formally notified, and less than half (28) were investigated by the Health Board social workers to the point of an interview with the parents/carers of the children concerned.

This compromise was reached by means of a number of unacknowledged filtering devices that were operated by the social workers. On examination it can be seen that some of these were linked more to the manner in which allegations were referred than to the perceived risk or danger inherent in the reports. It appears that child protection priorities were more organisational than child centred, with the balance tilted more towards discounting than endorsing the validity of allegations. For example: occasionally when referrals were made, particularly through a third party, the information relayed was not considered adequate to sustain a classification of child abuse even if the referrer identified it as such. The responsibility for ascertaining more evidence at these times was not borne by the duty social workers, but was left with the referrer. In one instance, a general practitioner telephoned the duty social worker because he had been 'informed' by a patient that some children related to her were at risk of sexual abuse from another relative, a 'known' abuser. He did not have the name or address of the family whose children were allegedly at risk and he was asked to call back with this information. He failed to do so, or to respond to messages and letters that were sent by the social workers to remind him. The case was eventually closed with no further action. This decision was reached without any reason to believe that the original allegation was untrue, but it was clear that, in the view of the social workers, the responsibility still lay with the referring general practitioner and it was presumed that he would make contact if he continued to have concerns.

In a similar situation, a probation officer had contacted the office to report an allegation of potential sexual abuse, and was asked to get back to his original source of information, a client of his, to clarify the facts. The client had intimated to the probation officer that her boyfriend's sister was being abused by her uncle. The duty social worker at the time felt it was something that warranted more information and investigation. The probation officer, however, failed to pursue the matter, and ultimately, the social work team in turn stopped pursuing him about it, once again operating in the normative belief that his lack of response diluted the gravity implied in the original referral and that if there was substance to the referral, he would have reacted more assertively.

Reports specifying child abuse were less likely to be endorsed by the social workers if they were from people with 'reputations' for making invalid referrals. One such allegation involved a child with an unkempt, unhealthy appearance, who was frequently absent from school and 'seemed frightened' in the presence of her mother. Concern about this child was reported to the duty social worker by a school principal who suggested that the little girl was 'emotionally and physically neglected'. This particular school principal was known to the social workers, several of whom had met him at case conferences. His reputation for impetuosity in reporting suspected, though rarely validated, child abuse caused them to feel sceptical about this referral. As one of them put it:

> …my experience of that man is that he rings up on the spur of the moment when he has something in his head. He starts hares running and then a few days later he's on to something else and he's forgotten about this…

In the event, the social work team did not act on the teacher's concerns but asked him to address the physical aspects of the child's neglect himself by providing meals and a uniform. Nor did they pursue another referral concerning a traveller woman who was out begging with her child, without shelter in very cold, wet weather. This was reported by a man who was known to have a very public concern, often voiced through the media, about the plight of children begging. It evoked an ambiguous response from the team and no further action was taken on the basis that the referrer had offered no real evidence of abuse and was unreliable and prone to exaggeration in order to accommodate his personal agenda.

Despite the explicit instruction in the child abuse guidelines that child abuse reports should be followed by an investigation, including an interview with parents/carers and a meeting with the child, this process did not always follow the entry of a 'child abuse/neglect' referral into the intake book. However, when observed in practice, the breaching of the guidelines could not be construed simply as a result of negligence or indifference. Failure by the workers to make the officially anticipated response can be more authentically explained by their *re-framing* of the original concern, the gravity of the incident and, as demonstrated above, the intention of the referring person or their responsibility for investigating it. This reconstruction was achieved by the workers, sometimes individually, though more often collectively at team meetings, through a re-contextualising of the events which preceded the agency contact, and was the result of a combination of elements which will be illustrated in the following sections.

Although the foregoing example of the A case illustrates the difficulty in determining thresholds for sexual abuse, the means of measuring the seriousness and the need for response in relation to suspected neglect appeared even more complex. A number of factors came into play, and again, much energy was dedicated to discounting levels of seriousness, thereby altering the 'abuse' definition and obviating the need to intervene by investigation. In common with other studies (Gibbons *et al.* 1995; Farmer and Owen 1995; Thorpe 1994; Buckley *et al.* 1997; Ferguson and O'Reilly 2001; Horwath 2001) the children who were referred to the social work team were, in the majority of cases (57%), cared for by lone parents, mostly mothers. In some instances, there was not sufficient information in the records to make an assessment of the parents' financial situations, but there was enough evidence to show that at least half of those referred were social welfare recipients. Although the proportion of families which were investigated for suspected child abuse was roughly equal for those of an 'employed' rather than an 'unemployed' status, there was evidence to show that reports of alleged neglect in families who had a history of ongoing problems such as addiction, poverty and psychiatric illness were less likely to be investigated.

For example, one of the factors that determined the appropriateness of a 'neglect' designation was the history of the family in question, and whether or not it was known to the social workers. This has been noted by Thorpe (1994) who views the consideration of a history in terms of a 'moralising' activity practised by workers, which in this instance, includes consideration of the families' willingness to change. However, rather than making harsher judgements and stronger interventions where families were known to be unco-operative, the social workers in Ballyowen tended to discount referrals about them, unless the reported behaviours appeared so extreme that intervention was inevitable (e.g. if a child was abandoned, or seriously injured, or received into care). These judgements were influenced by a combination of pessimism about the value of intervention, and ambivalence about the boundaries between poor quality care and 'neglect', in a context of general adversity where it was felt that an accusation of child abuse would further undermine the carers' already stretched parenting capacities, a trend also identified by Stevenson (1998) in a later UK study.

When patterns of investigation,[5] are examined, this trend appears to continue. Twenty-eight (39%) of the families on whom this case study is based had been previously reported to the social workers in Ballyowen because of concerns about their children. When they were re-referred during the fieldwork period for this study, just under half of them were either not investigated, or the follow up was devolved to another agency. Nine of these referrals concerned alleged child neglect, one emotional abuse and three involved sexual abuse allegations. Of the neglect referrals, six had common elements of poverty and histories of chronic neglect, and two concerned parents with a psychiatric illness; there was also substance abuse in two that was constant but did not attract particular attention. A child and family centre was involved with one case, and was asked to follow up the concern. In another case, a seven and four-year-old were found alone in their house by a non-Health Board professional who was visiting in the course of his work. He was asked by the duty social worker to deal with the incident in the course of his other work with the family. Other specific concerns included a child suffering alleged emotional and physical neglect, two reports of general neglect due to parental drug-taking, 'suspicious' behaviour between a child and an older man, and a child who was 'neglected looking with dirty clothes…tired and wanting to sleep', who had been the subject of reports many times before and who the school were asked to follow up.

Although it was not explicitly stated by the social workers, their response suggested that the variable connecting these referrals was a sense of hopelessness about what could be achieved by intervening. The emotional abuse referral concerned a 16-year-old with an 'alcoholic' mother. The initial call had been made by a concerned neighbour who then put the child on to the phone to talk to the social worker. The child had stated that she didn't want social workers 'barging in' and claimed that she had friends and supports in the neighbourhood. The sexual abuse reports contained what was regarded as insufficient identifying information in one case, were made in the context of a marital dispute in the second, and in the third case, a treatment agency already working with the family was asked to follow up the alleged concern.

Of the 17 previously known families who *were* investigated, there were concerns about sexual abuse in seven, seven others concerned neglect, and three physical abuse. There were considerable differences between the 'previously known' neglect allegations that were not investigated, and the 'previously known' neglect allegations that were. In the latter category, two reports concerned children where the mothers had drink problems and whose behaviour attracted a lot of attention, three were 'chronic' but with other professionals actively involved, one was from a middle class neighbourhood where the neglect was more visible, and in the last case, a child was left abandoned so there was no option for the social work service but to become involved. The three physical abuse allegations which were investigated in families that were previously known also had aspects that seemed to compel a response: in one case facial bruising was reported by another agency, and another family had a history of Munchausen's syndrome by proxy. In the third case, the complaint was one of several which were made by the mother's estranged partner and presumed to be false, but it was felt by the social work team that she had a right to hear about it. The fact that a higher proportion of sexual abuse allegations were investigated reflects the normal response to such referrals whether they were previously known or not (Gibbons *et al.* 1995; Cleaver and Freeman 1995, Buckley *et al.* 1997).

Cultural relativism in operation

These findings suggest that reports about families who were previously known to the social work team in Ballyowen were likely to be 'endorsed' as child abuse, and re-investigated, if they concerned sexual abuse or highly visible neglect, or physical abuse where there were strong reasons to suspect it was non-accidental. The active involvement of agencies outside the statutory system also appeared to precipitate the categorisation of the concern as 'abuse', reflecting a process termed 'failure of agency containment', a phrase originally coined by Dingwall *et al.* (1983). The case examples also serve to illustrate how debates about the definition of child maltreatment, particularly neglect, are frequently conducted with reference to cultural norms. The operation of 'cultural relativism'[6] (Dingwall *et al.* 1983) was implicitly acknowledged by the social workers as an influence on their own ability to discriminate between what was abuse or not. It tended to work both ways, for example, a report of children being left playing outside an apartment block all day in a middle class area was entered in the intake book as 'child abuse/neglect', yet one practitioner observed: 'if they were in [a local authority flat complex] nobody would notice that they were unsupervised'.

Reports of non-national children who were apparently without beds and sleeping on the floor, were examined in terms of their own culture: 'I wouldn't be concerned about whether the children are sleeping on the floor...that's the way they construct their own lifestyle...their own cultural preference...'. Reports of a very young lone mother's questionable ability to mind her child were debated by workers at the team meeting, and a social worker expressed her ambivalence about it in these terms:

> While the conditions in which the child might be left mightn't be great, whether you'd call it neglect, or whether it's just a different social value system than either the caller or ourselves would feel appropriate...it's hard to know.

Neither of the last two referrals was investigated. Dingwall *et al* (1983) have offered examples of the way cultural relativism operated in relation to racial or minority ethnic groups. The example of the non-national family just quoted fits into this category, but given the as yet low level of multi-racialism in Ireland compared to other countries, such occurrences are relatively rare. However, traveller families consistently feature in Health Board statistics of various types, and they constitute a group whose culture is viewed as uniquely different from the general population. Poor health and high levels of infant mortality among the travellers have been documented, and it is known that Irish traveller children are more likely to die from accidents, suffer from congenital defects and are more likely than other children to be admitted to care (Task Force on the Travelling Community 1995). Yet, examination of the response to child abuse concerning travellers in this study indicates a lot of fluidity in terms of the adjudication of 'risk' and good enough parenting. Paradoxically, their very visible and alternative lifestyle seemed to obscure differentiation between normal standards and neglect, and there was a very liberal acceptance of questionable parenting practices where they occurred. For example, when a report was made by a member of the public who was concerned about a very young traveller child begging 'in all weathers', the social worker made a quite ambivalent response: 'What would signify a neglect situation? If the child is properly covered when it's raining is she neglected then?'

The challenging nature of child protection work with travellers has since been illustrated in the literature (Cemlyn 2000). However, social workers in Ballyowen were aware of, but did not particularly address, their difficulties in assessing parenting standards in traveller families, either in practice, or in their interviews with me. One of the reports described a rather bleak-sounding situation, where a 14-year-old traveller girl was found by a Garda in a cold, dirty house at night, minding nine siblings including a four-month-old infant whom she couldn't feed properly because she didn't have a teat on the bottle. The attitude of the duty social worker that took the report was coloured by her knowledge of the complexities involved in applying traditional standards to alternative lifestyles:

> Yes…it's because they're from a different culture that different child care standards are applied…and that it's not straightforward…it's very difficult to set up an alternative care situation which is going to work for them, in the settled community.

As well as pointing out the ambivalence associated with the operation of culturally relativist perspectives by the workers, these findings indicate that a significant obstacle to the application of the 'child abuse' label was the (un)likelihood of successful intervention. It was commonly believed that there was little point in investigating something that may be denied by the carers, as one of the social workers pointed out: '...the issue is if you are going to pick up these things, whether you can do anything with them.'

The ongoing debate about physical punishment was reflected in social workers' frustration, particularly when there were other issues involved, like poverty and stress. A social worker investigating a report about 'slapping' expressed some reservations:

> Slapping... I have question marks...I don't know if I'm the best person to be going out to see this woman...I don't know whether I should be going out at all! ...we find it very difficult to distinguish between hitting a child for reasons of discipline and beating them up.

Social workers' avoidance of violent men

In the same way as families which appeared to have 'chronic' difficulties (and by definition, did not display much capacity to change) were less likely to be subject to interventions, those where a history of aggressive or criminal behaviour was present, particularly if the perpetrator was a man, appeared to be filtered out fairly readily. This finding appears to be in keeping with Milner's (1993, 1996) and Daniel and Taylor's (2001) theories about practitioners' avoidance and mitigation of violent men. For example, a public health nurse contacted the duty social worker to report that an 18-month-old child, in the sole care of his father, allegedly had a large bruise on his face. The neighbour who had referred the matter to the nurse had described the father as 'a right bowzy...a well-known criminal in the area'. The child's mother, who had left the family home, was a drug user, and the father apparently suffered from full blown AIDS as well as a drug problem, and engaged in crime to finance his habit. The public health nurse had, in fact, visited in response to the neighbour's allegation, but she did not mention the reported concerns to the father. The nurse told the social worker that she was 'scared out of her wits' visiting the home because of what she knew about the father. She had not observed any bruising on the child's face at the time, and on that basis, the referral was closed.

Out of the 39 lone parents involved in the child abuse referrals, four were male, including the one just described. One of the other three was actually out of the country at the time the report was made, and therefore could not be contacted, but neither of the other two was contacted either. One man had a reputation for involvement with a paramilitary organisation in Northern Ireland. The other man, who was reported twice, allegedly had a drink problem that made him violent and aggressive. As in the first case mentioned, duty social workers sought information about these families via third parties rather than personal interview.

The matter of 'responsibility' for referral of child abuse in relation to the reporting behaviour of some professionals has already been mentioned and the threshold beyond which the Health Board social workers refused to go in pursuance of information when other professionals were not particularly forthcoming has been identified. The issues of inter-agency and inter-professional relationships and co-ordination permeated the practice of statutory social workers to such an extent that they need to be examined at several stages, and will reappear at different points in the book.

Inter-professional and inter-agency co-operation at the early stages of child protection

The 1987 Child Abuse Guidelines which were operational at the time the fieldwork was conducted suggest that co-operation is not just the business of social workers, public health nurses and area medical officers, but depends on the 'ready willingness and co-operation' of medical personnel, the police, schools and non-statutory agencies. The 'co-ordinating' role required of the aforementioned professionals is not specified, and the interpretations ascribed to it by themselves and by the statutory social workers were often widely divergent, giving rise to quite bitter resentments.

The Health Board social workers tended to operate on the assumption that agencies which were involved over a period with children, had engaged with the families, or had a good knowledge of the home situation, should also carry some responsibility for, or at least share, the investigation of child abuse concerns which arose in the course of their work with the families. The delegation of investigation to other agencies had a recognised function, to provide an initial filtering process, which might reduce pressure on the social work team, leaving them to get on with 'serious' work as described by one of the social workers:

> A lot of stuff comes to us that maybe could be diverted before it gets here because some of it is very clearly simply people's anxieties and there's no basis for it.

No clear policy existed, however, and there was a history in Ballyowen of tension between certain agencies. Dingwall *et al.* (1983) have reported on the propensity of 'failure of agency containment' to heighten the possibility of statutory intervention. By this, they meant that once professional involvement breached the boundaries of the primary group, that is, the social work team, or local authority, by the involvement of another agency or perhaps the police, it was more likely that a report of child abuse would be actively pursued, as the statutory agency would be more self-conscious of its obligations and its image. The latter effect was observable at times in this study, but was overshadowed by disagreement about which agency should carry out the investigative interview, reflecting a notion proposed by Butler (1996) that non-social work professionals in Ireland can be reluctant to take on the social policing 'mantle'.

The root of some of the inter-agency difficulties, in line with Butler's (1996) observations, seemed to lie in the perception of the Health Board social workers that they tended to be left with the difficult, confrontative elements of the work, and that other agencies wanted to do 'therapy in isolation', avoiding the 'unpleasant, confrontative, action taking bits'. The Health Board social workers believed that this was not only unfair, but that it contravened good practice rules. They also resented the implication that 'co-ordination' meant them taking responsibility for the 'nasty' bits to facilitate the treatment agencies doing the 'nice' work:

> ...it's an expectation that we will hold their hands while they are doing it...or they would hold our hands while we give the nasty noises and they sit in the background and make the sweet noises...

Wise (1989) observes a contradiction inherent in the official assumption that child abuse is the responsibility of social workers, while at the same time, social workers are constantly urged to share this responsibility with others. In a similar vein, the notion of co-operation, as suggested in guidance and policy documents, was regarded with some cynicism by the Health Board workers in this study, as one of them put it:

> People keep saying we can only do it with the co-operation of other agencies, but I mean other agencies seem to see their co-operation in a different way than the Health Board do.

Several instances of poor inter-agency work manifested themselves in the initial period of processing referrals, the impact of these differences being serious enough to deflect attention away from the children and families who were the subjects of the referrals. For example, in one case, a treatment service had been working with a seven-year-old child and his parents for two years over his behavioural difficulties. At a particular point the agency became worried about the child's physical safety in his home, and they requested a Health Board social worker to carry out a risk assessment with them. The Health Board duty social worker responded that as the treatment agency employed social workers and knew the family well, they were in a better position to carry out the assessment. This resulted in a stand-off between the agencies, and no co-operation ensued. The treatment agency's concerns grew stronger and the child was eventually received into Health Board care for his own protection. Unfortunately, the urgency with which this was executed left little room for making the process any easier for the little boy, and his entry into care was quite sudden and traumatic. Following this incident, a Health Board social worker acknowledged the way that poor inter-agency co-operation between professionals was impacting on families, particularly the child in this case:

> He was so confused, the poor little thing… I think there needs to be a closer liaison between outside agencies that we get referrals from…there's a mistrust between us at the moment and I think that…we try not to get involved, and the loser is the child, and it doesn't make it any easier…this stand-off thing at the end of the day doesn't make it any easier. Because someone has to end up then going out on a mercy basis, and trying to pick it up, it's just crazy…

Paradoxically, while medical social workers and social workers in voluntary agencies were very much encouraged by the Health Board/statutory social workers to carry out initial investigations, it was acknowledged by the statutory social workers that the same norms might not necessarily apply:

> ...we end up hanging up the phone feeling that an agency is going to do something specific, and the agency hang up with a totally different idea, so we're both...because our expectations are one thing and theirs are something else...and we never check it out and we both honestly hang up thinking we have a handle on it, and we don't, you know...

Nevertheless, despite the fact that there was no guarantee of uniform practices, the abrogation of responsibility for investigation to agencies outside the Health Board was a common means of the disposal of referrals.

The 'duty' system for receiving reports of suspected child abuse

The previous section has highlighted the avoidance of engagement with child protection work demonstrated by non-statutory agencies. There were other examples in the study of the way that certain norms adopted by statutory workers acted strategically to ensure that responsibility remained with other agencies. What is commonly known as the 'duty' system,[7] referred to earlier, is one example of this. As the earlier part of this chapter inferred, each day, in the area where the research was conducted, a social worker was 'on duty' to receive referrals and take telephone calls from outside professionals and members of the public. This would be normal practice in most Health Board areas. All emergency matters would be dealt with on the same day, but many of the cases referred could be either non-specific in terms of the risk implied, or lacking in evidence. As a consequence, there would frequently be occasions where further clarification or assessment was needed or information was not readily available. In the context of more urgent tasks to be completed, either in relation to 'duty' or in his or her long-term caseload, the duty social worker might not have time to deal with it immediately. In that case, at the end of the day, he or she would pass the duty file to next day's duty worker, who would also have been carrying long-term cases in addition to emergency work.

Consequently, if the response to a child abuse referral was being carried over several days, it was necessary for different social workers to gather more detail, often from the same referring person. This sometimes caused considerable frustration to referring professionals who, having to repeat the same information to different workers, perceived that they were either not being taken seriously, or were being 'fobbed off'.

While it was never consciously identified by statutory social workers as a means of diffusing ownership or responsibility, the practice of passing duty matters between different workers could be compared to a process identified in a much earlier but still very relevant organisational study conducted by Menzies (1970). In a study which examined staff behaviour in a hospital setting, Menzies identified what she termed 'ritual defensive behaviours' and strict adherence to procedures adopted by professionals in stressful or uncertain circumstances. In her study, she noted how nurses could protect and distance themselves from potentially unpredictable or emotionally demanding situations by, for example, depersonalising patients and referring to them by their illnesses rather than their names, thus avoiding close involvement.

A comparison could be made between the type of ritual behaviour evident in Menzies' research and the 'duty' system in this study whereby social workers carried out routine assessment work, but the act of passing on the referral to others meant that it was not 'owned' by an individual worker. It was suggested by a referring psychologist that the apparent diffusion of work was a deliberate ploy:

> I wondered was it policy to do this so that nobody could get into it in any depth, so it meant that [the Health Board] would stay superficially involved…as they just put somebody in different every day into it…

Whatever the intention of the Health Board workers, their intake procedures contributed considerably to tension between themselves and other agencies that sought a statutory response to child protection concerns. Research has shown that this type of practice is common in situations where escalating demands and inadequate resources force practitioners to prioritise their own survival and ration the number of cases they accept, and is particularly prevalent where practitioners feel under-valued and misunderstood (Wise 1989; Morrison 1996; Scott 1997).

Ideological contradictions in child protection work

The statutory social workers' irritation at the way they perceived other services selectively fragmenting situations into Health Board business and 'nice work' reflected a lot of their own frustration about their obligation to investigate abuse. However, the accounts which have been given here of the devices employed to minimise the amount of investigative activity belie their belief that they were acting in an interventive, 'policing' fashion. That they had this 'heavy' image of themselves was demonstrated by statements such as this one made by one of the social workers:

> ...every allegation that comes in we have to go out after and we have to check it out...you are checking out every tiny little thing in case you miss something and just in case something might go wrong tomorrow or six months time and somebody will come back to you and you will be pinned to the wall, whatever professional judgement you have made or haven't made, or anything...its almost like you are walking on a tight-rope, and we're taking it on...it's giving us a very bad image...social workers are going to be seen in a particular light...getting excited about every little smack...have they nothing better to be doing...

The social workers were aware that despite a 'public' ideology about children's welfare and safety, individuals resented intrusions into their private lives. As one worker claimed:

> People on television and things will always say, well if the social workers have any suspicion about me, well of course they must come around and check me out. But I mean, when you actually do it that's not the response that you get.

Yet, as the case examples have shown, despite the self-perception of the social workers as being intrusive and heavy handed, considerable flexibility was actually used in decision-making about which referrals warranted investigation. The fact that under half of the reported allegations resulted in an interview with the child or children's carers is testimony to the non-interventionist philosophy that operated. However, the workers themselves did not appear to be conscious of the discretion that they exercised in relation to the disposal of referrals. There was a strong perception that they were constrained by a number of factors into a narrow, proceduralised type of practice. In fact, the tensions around what the workers perceived to be their unwarrantedly intrusive activities could be seen to contrast with the strategies they actually employed to keep their workload manageable, minimise the 'heaviness' of their interventions, and as much as possible, devolve or at least share the responsibility for the 'dirty work' of child protection amongst other agencies and professionals. The following section will illustrate this point.

'Notification' of child abuse

The proportion of referred allegations of child abuse/neglect in this study that were formally notified to the Director of Community Care was low, given the clear directive in the guidelines. Out of the 72 allegations reported, 18[8] made it to the notification stage, that is, the formal process of filling out notification forms and sending them up the line. Fourteen of the notifications were made by the Ballyowen social workers, one by a public health nurse, two by police officers, and one by a senior manager from another Health Board area. Although the Ballyowen social workers had no control over the notification or otherwise of the last four, which by-passed them and went straight to the Director, the decision to notify the first 14 was theirs.

When I asked the social workers what the process of 'notification' meant to them, their replies varied. One worker saw it as a bureaucratic exercise: 'it becomes part of a system, whereby there are checks and balances and certain procedures that have to be followed'. Another worker perceived the process as a way of introducing accountability into the system:

> The Director is informed, and there's more sort of formal discussion about the cases which means that more attention is given to the cases than if it's just left to yourself, so a more responsible attitude is taken.

Notification was also seen as an insurance against inaction: 'It goes into the system which means it's not going to go astray, and it's going to be followed up…it's a way of sharing responsibility'. So, social workers freely acknowledged the significance of taking the procedural step of notifying cases as far as their own accountability was concerned. They also appreciated, however, the seriousness of this process for the subjects involved. Notifying a case meant intruding a little further into family privacy, and the following statement exemplifies the social workers' unease with this process:

> It's one step further than having a file on the family...it's one thing having a record, but it's very different having it on a register. Purely from a civil rights point of view, if people are on lists, they should know.

There was no formal 'register' as such, though the Director did keep a list of children who had been notified. The list itself appeared to have no particular purpose other than to provide a record for reviewing the processing of child abuse allegations. The removal of names from the list was not a particularly significant event and parents were not specifically made aware of the list's existence. However, several of the social workers mentioned it while talking about the business of notifying, and even called it the 'register' although it was never referred to as such by management. Their concern about the seriousness of notifying cases made practitioners hesitant to take that step. Some preferred to wait for a degree of certainty, suggesting that they don't like 'putting things into the system until you are more sure about them' and resisting notification 'if there was nothing but rumour or speculation or nothing substantial'. Although notifying a case was not necessarily synonymous with pursuing an investigation, the social workers clearly saw it as a 'heavy' action to take. It seemed to serve an important function, and in order to preserve its importance, they were anxious not to devalue it, as expressed by a worker:

> I would see it as to ensure that the thing is followed up quickly...to establish whether any action is needed to be taken to protect the child...but in order to achieve that, if you then overload the system, or you start putting through things that are essentially not 'risk' situations, then the whole procedure becomes devalued, and people don't really put much weight upon it.

The added accountability implied by having a family's name on the list meant obligatory visits, according to a worker who was sceptical about the value of spending time this way. As she put it:

> To workers, it means that very often you're involved in a monitoring role where you may not be very effective but you feel you have to stick in there in a monitoring fashion...

It became obvious that the social workers were using their powers of selectivity at a crucial stage in the processing of child abuse referrals, the part where a decision had to be made about whether or not to 'notify'. It must be pointed out here that this research was conducted prior to the full implementation of the Child Care Act 1991, which could explain what might be seen as a discretionary response to child protection concerns. A study carried out in 1996/7 in the Mid-Western Health Board region of Ireland showed that just under half (169 out of 319) child care concerns were referred to the child protection notification system in that area, illustrating a fairly conservative approach in comparison (Ferguson and O'Reilly 2001). It is also pertinent that under *Children First*, the national child protection guidelines published in 1999, notification systems have been standardised across the health boards, undoubtedly streamlining and thereby modifying their usage. However, notwithstanding these changes, the threshold of decision-making about notification still remains a very crucial one and the interplay of various and conflicting norms and values combine to sustain its controversial nature. This was the last point at which front-line practitioners could retain control over the management of their work. As has been demonstrated, they used a combination of what sometimes appeared like contradictory criteria to assist them in 'gate-keeping' the system. Yet, they rarely explicitly acknowledged the scale of discretion that they employed, and it is questionable whether they were actually aware of it.

Conclusion

This chapter has reported and critically analysed the research data regarding the first steps taken by Health Board social workers in operationalising their duty to respond to allegations of child abuse and neglect. It has demonstrated, with many examples, that social workers may not at all times be willing to: first, recognise concerns reported to them as 'abuse' and, second, to enter those concerns into the official system. Thus, it can be observed that the assumptions underpinning the official guidance do not readily translate into the sort of responses that are implied. In fact, the way in which such concepts as 'risk', 'neglect' and child sexual abuse are situationally constructed reflects a contrasting operational paradigm. There is a great deal of evidence in the literature that, in an uncertain context such as that in which social work and child protection are situated, 'sense-making' is applied by practitioners (Pithouse 1987; Wise 1989; Parton *et al.* 1997). This chapter has begun to demonstrate how such activity operates in relation to recognition and categorisation of child abuse, and to explain some of the factors that comprise the framework within which decision-making operates. As I have suggested, in many respects the discussion so far has been more concerned with the techniques used to *eliminate* potential cases from the system than it has with the processes of actively responding to child abuse reports. Yet, as Thorpe (1997) points out, an increasing proportion of the work of child protection is concerned with unsubstantiated reports. This chapter has, therefore, legitimately focused attention on an activity that occupies a considerable proportion of the work of child protection.

Thorpe (1994) found that despite the 'unwritten assumption in the literature that the identification of "risk" or neglect or the substantiation of abuse automatically triggers intervention', such a response cannot be assumed. His finding is replicated in this study. Less than half the allegations of abuse, that is half of the referrals that were entered into the 'child abuse/neglect' category at intake, were investigated by the Health Board social workers in their statutory capacity. However, even though the rate of investigation was inconsistent, the *nature* and *purpose* of investigation did fit into a pattern of activities, which combined to produce a particular type of adjudication. The next chapter will illustrate the processes involved.

Endnotes

1 I use the term 'Health Board' to indicate that not all referrals were made to the social work team, some of them having been first directed to the Director of Community Care/senior area medical officer.

2 Referrals are 'notified' when they are officially reported in writing (usually, though not always, on specially designed forms) to the senior area medical officer or Director of Community Care. As this chapter shows, 'notification' was not always carried out by the social workers who processed child abuse/neglect reports.

3 The unit of analysis here is one child. There may have been more than one child identified in each referral.

4 All the names used in this study, of places, persons or agencies have been changed.

5 That is, when a decision was made to actually meet with parents or carers.

6 Cultural relativism is explained by Dingwall *et al.* (1983) as a type of 'rule' according to which members of one culture could not justifiably criticise members of another by employing their own normative standards. Dingwall et al. identified some examples of ethnic status being used to justify deviant conduct, e.g. the beating of West Indian children being justified by viewing it in terms of its traditional use as a punishment within that culture.

7 In all Health Board areas there is a social worker 'on duty' to receive referrals and take telephone calls from outside professionals and members of the public. Some areas now operate duty teams, where the same staff cover duty all the time, and only pass on cases to the rest of the team when it is considered necessary to allocate them for long-term work. Even with this arrangement, it is frequently the case that different workers are on duty each day, which means that no one person takes responsibility for a case until it is allocated.

8 The 18 reports concerned 33 children, constituting 33 notifications, out of a potential 144 notifications arising from the total of 72 reports made.

Chapter Three

Making Sense of the Evidence
Assessment of Child Protection Concerns

The framework made visible in this study, through which child abuse allegations are 'constructed' by local authority/Health Board social workers, was considered in the previous chapter. It described the manner in which referrals made by either professionals or members of the public are screened in such a way as to affirm or discount the 'child abuse' status that had been provisionally assigned to them. A circular relationship, linking the validity of their classification with the necessity to investigate the reported allegations, was demonstrated. If a report survived the initial filtering process, it was deemed to have been correctly categorised as 'child abuse'. Via this process, it was endorsed as warranting further enquiry. On the other hand, if a report was not considered worth investigating, its original designation was nullified. As the case examples demonstrated, referrals which did not fit the 'text-book' versions suggested by the child abuse procedures were subjected by the social workers to a type of sense-making that reached an often fragile consensus. Such a screening process has no place in the official discourse of child protection, but as this study confirms, in reality, it constitutes much of the 'work' involved.

This chapter now examines the next step in the child protection process, the assessment of evidence gained at the investigative stage. This account will attempt to explain the adjudication process from the 'actor's' perspective, that is, through the voices of the social work practitioners, in the context within which they were operating. As the previous chapter has demonstrated, 28 of the 72 reports initially categorised as 'child abuse/neglect' were followed up by the statutory social workers to the point of an interview with parent/s, including two investigations of one family who were reported twice. The other 44 were disposed of in various ways for different reasons. In eight instances, the decision not to follow up was influenced by the absence of either the address or identity of the children deemed at risk, efforts made to trace them having been unsuccessful. The families identified in two other referrals had permanent addresses outside the catchment area, so the responsibility for follow up was passed on to the relevant office. Twenty-one were closed with no investigation beyond preliminary telephone checks, generally because the weight of evidence gained at that stage was not considered sufficient to warrant any further enquiry.

Thirteen allegations were 'investigated' by professionals other than statutory social workers, three by police officers, three by social workers working in treatment agencies, three by public health nurses, three by medical social workers, and one by a social worker from a voluntary agency for children with physical disabilities. The delegation of this duty to professionals outside the statutory sector was normally determined by a judgement, first, that the concerns may well be unfounded, and second, that these particular professionals were in a better position to get information, either because they were already working with the families who were implicated, or they had easier access to them. It also served the purpose of reducing the workload of the statutory social workers and satisfying them that the responsibility for 'dirty work', that is, the investigation of child abuse, was being shared by other child care professionals.

However, as the previous chapter has shown, no efforts were made to standardise the type of investigation to be carried out by any of the agencies involved. As it turned out, of the 13 allegations followed up by professionals who were not statutory social workers, three were kept 'open' to their own agencies as child protection cases, and no further action was recommended in the other ten situations. The high rate of closure in this group of referrals could be explained from two perspectives: one, that the statutory social workers showed correct discrimination in delegating the investigation as, given the low rate of substantiation involved, it saved them time and protected the families from Health Board intervention, a process which the social workers believed to be traumatic. On the other hand, given the differential judgements applied to child care issues by different professionals (Giovannoni and Becerra 1979), it is possible that quite different standards were used in reaching these assessments. Equally, what Dingwall *et al.* (1983) termed the 'division of regulatory labour' that serves to fragment the professional perspectives applied, could have reduced the likelihood of identifying dangerous or harmful situations.

There was a discernible pattern in the responses made to different types of abuse. As the previous chapter has indicated, 'investigation' is here defined as an activity that involves, at the very least, a personal interview with the parents and/or children implicated in the referral. Of the 21 'sexual abuse' referrals, 13 were investigated (57%). Of the 34 'neglect' referrals, eight were investigated (24%). Seven of the thirteen 'physical abuse' referrals were investigated (46%), and none of the reports of 'emotional abuse'. This data replicates Gibbons *et al.*'s (1995) finding that child protection referrals were more likely to be filtered out without investigation if they concerned emotional abuse or neglect rather than physical abuse or child sexual abuse. Reports of sexual abuse evoked a stronger reaction than the others. In nine of the 21 sexual abuse allegations, children themselves had disclosed the abuse. While these referrals were not always substantiated, they were always investigated. A far lower proportion of neglect allegations were investigated, suggesting that it is a harder concept to define and separate from other factors that did not fit as comfortably into the 'abuse' framework. A later Irish study has confirmed that this trend persists (Horwath 2001).

The most crucial sites for assessment of child abuse reports were, first, the parental interview, which was often combined with meeting the child or children involved, and second, the case conference. This chapter will deal mainly with the first of these. The outcomes of the investigative interview and assessment of the information gathered could be divided into two categories: a decision to take no further action and a decision to allocate the case for further child protection work including a possible case conference and further assessment. There was also a sub-category for the further disposal of cases, which was to transfer or relegate them to the voluntary agencies with whom they were already involved with the expectation that child protection would form part of the working brief of the agencies with the families concerned.

Focus on mothers

There is ample evidence in the literature of the tendency for child protection practitioners to focus on mothers, even when the abuser is a father or father figure (Farmer and Owen 1995; Milner 1993, 1996; O' Hagan and Dillenberger 1995; Daniel and Taylor 2001; Horwath 2001). This study replicates those findings, particularly when the investigative interview is considered. Fourteen of the families who were the subject of investigative interviews were headed by a lone parent, in all cases the mother. In nine of these, there featured some sort of ongoing relationship between the mother and a man who had regular and frequent contact with the children. In some instances, the man was either a cohabitee or non-resident partner of the mother's; in others he was the children's father, estranged from the mother, but still in frequent contact. In only one of these situations was the man interviewed as part of the investigation, despite the fact that in four family situations, two of which were reported twice, the partners or former partners were strongly implicated in the reported incident.

In the 14 other families that were headed by two parents, the mother only was seen in eight instances, and fathers were not included in any part of the investigation even though they were the alleged abusers in four of these situations. These findings affirm Milner's (1993, 1996) theory regarding child protection workers' avoidance of violent men, but also highlight the taken-for-granted notion that child care is the mother's job, supporting theories in the literature about the gendered division of child-related work in households (Daniel and Taylor 2001; Edwards 1998; Farmer and Owen 1995; Milner 1993; C. Parton 1990). This point is well illustrated in one instance where a referral was being investigated. The social worker made a very deliberate decision to invite both parents to the office together to discuss the report, which had indicated that this mother, who was quite burdened with child care tasks, sometimes left her two very young children for long periods on their own while she went out. However, the social worker made it very plain that the purpose of the father's presence was to support the mother in dealing with the complaint about her care of the children, and to make sure she understood the gravity of the situation:

> I figured that it was really important for both the husband and wife to be seen together…important that the mother shouldn't be seen on her own because…we don't know how much she would be able to hear…

Essentially in this case, the husband's presence at the interview was used to assist the social worker in her assessment of the mother's parenting skills, inasmuch as he was more or less asked if he was satisfied with his wife's care of the children. This is illustrated by the social worker's later statement: '…the husband was saying that he comes home most dinner times because he works close, and has never witnessed this, and if he had, he wouldn't let it go on'.

Milner (1993) suggests that the use of the word 'parents' in official documents is quite misleading, as most of the questions are specifically geared towards mothers. In this regard, my use of the word 'parents' and 'mother' in this book could be misconstrued. The majority of parents involved with the child protection system under analysis were mothers; for that reason, I have used the word 'mother' instead of 'parents' where the facts being discussed apply to mothers only. My use of the word 'mother' is not intended to impute any notion that mothers are solely responsible for the parenting of children, or to enforce any notion that child protection investigations should be conducted only with mothers.

In addition to the invisibility of fathers in child protection investigations, it is particularly interesting to note that despite the requirement in the child abuse guidelines in operation at the time to 'see the child and note and assess appearance and behaviour' (Department of Health 1987, p.11), the child or children who were the subjects of concern were seen in relation to only 17 of the 28 investigated cases. This finding can be taken to infer that whatever the nature of the other enquiries carried out, their focus was certainly not on the 'appearance and behaviour' of the children. In six of the investigations where the children were present, the social workers told me that they had seen them only because they happened to be there at the parental interview, but they had not specifically set out to see them, nor did they spend much time evaluating either their physical condition, or their views on the child protection concern which led to the interview. This finding provides confirmation of Parton *et al.*'s (1997) observations about the absence of children in child protection work and Horwath's (2001) later finding in an Irish study that meaningful engagement between child protection workers and children occurs in only a minority of cases. It is one that will become clearer when the grounds for assessment are made visible as this chapter develops.

It was normal practice for the social worker that had done the investigative interview to report his or her findings to the team meeting, together with a recommendation that was rarely challenged by their colleagues. I interviewed the social workers after they had done the initial investigative interview, and their answers, together with the discussions that normally followed at the team meetings, gave a picture of the areas that they had examined, and their own assessment of the information gleaned.

Assessment criteria and mitigating factors

When the investigations carried out in Ballyowen were explored, there was no impression of social workers doing formalised risk assessments and very little sense of their use of theory, for example, concepts about child development or family dynamics, or predictive checklists. In situations where there was a recorded history of previous incidents such as a child being in care, or a long involvement with the agency because of neglect, these factors were taken into consideration. Otherwise social workers appeared to approach investigations with open minds as to the validity of the allegation and the focus was very much on the reported incident rather than on the child and family's general situation.

The criteria that appear to have been used to assess the information gleaned from interviews were very much based on what Dingwall *et al.* (1983) would term 'social evidence', that is, the family's material environment and interpersonal relationships, particularly mother/child. There were, in fact, virtually no incidents where 'clinical' evidence in the form of an injury or mark to the child was the sole or principal source of suspicion. More common were reports from parents and in one case from a child, of sexual abuse; reports by neighbours, acquaintances or other 'interested parties' that they had witnessed children being hit or treated aggressively, or had witnessed or suspected that children had been left on their own, unsupervised. The latter were the disputable forms of evidence that were measured against a range of 'social' criteria, while the former, the allegations reported by the parents themselves, were generally judged in relation to the children's current 'safety' and the parent/s' ability to maintain it. Compliance, particularly from mothers as they were the parents most often interviewed, was viewed as significant, and in line with Dingwall *et al.*'s (1983, p.92) theory, that 'as long as parents maintained at least a surface co-operation they were less likely to be the object of compulsory action'. Also crucial was the mother's ability to accept and understand the meaning of the alleged concern for her child or children and indications of her willingness to protect, particularly in relation to child sexual abuse.

Notwithstanding the common variable of 'social' factors, the type of assessments applied by practitioners in this study varied according to the nature of the concerns reported. Within each category of abuse, the investigations had distinct elements that made them different from the others. For example, with regard to allegations of sexual abuse, seven were 'confirmed' to the extent that it was agreed by both parents and the investigating social worker that something of a sexual nature had occurred with their children, or in one case with a relative's children some years ago. When this was established, with the exception of the M case (detailed in the previous chapter), it was because the parent/s had discovered it or been told about it first and had reported it to social services, usually through another professional. In the aforementioned M case, the victim, a teenage girl, had disclosed it herself. Confirmation in these instances did not, therefore, come about as a result of forensic style investigations. Decisions regarding all of the 'unsubstantiated' sexual abuse allegations were reached on the basis of interviews with the mothers and in one case the child, but not the alleged perpetrators. Four of these allegations had been made by mothers against their children's fathers, one by a mother against an older brother of her child and one by neighbours against a child's mother and uncle. There was, in actual fact, little dispute involved, as the mothers were all co-operative and accepting of the social worker's assessment. Interestingly, four of these referrals were kept open for longer term intervention and the focus of work became 'welfare' as opposed to 'abuse' concerns. This may have some connection with the mothers' openness to working with the social work service but, as the previous chapter has shown, it is also virtually certain that they would not have been 'eligible' for a social work service had they not entered the system via the 'abuse' path.

When it came to investigations of physical abuse, assessments became slightly less clear-cut. Two of the allegations investigated were against persons outside the child's immediate family, in one instance, a care worker and in another, the child's estranged father. In both of these, the investigative interview was held with the mother, not the alleged perpetrator. Four physical abuse allegations were against mothers only. One was made anonymously about a parent who had been 'falsely' reported before. The validity of the allegation was doubted by the social worker, thus the mother was 'informed' rather than investigated. The other three were discussed with the mothers, two of whom claimed that they had lost control in response to their children's unmanageable behaviour. One of the investigations had included a medical examination that confirmed bruising consistent with the child being pushed against a hard surface, but as the mother had readily admitted it, the 'clinical' evidence was not crucial. The third mother denied that she was carrying out anything other than normal discipline (slapping her son). Three of the physical abuse referrals were allocated to Health Board social workers for further work, the one involving the estranged father, and the two with behavioural problems. The child whose mother admitted hurting him was received into short-term voluntary care and the ongoing work was shared between the Health Board social work service and the treatment service that had originally referred the case.

It was in relation to the referrals where neglect was the primary concern that most disputes arose in relation to the validity of the 'abuse' categorisation, and the social workers' ambivalence about the value of child protection investigations became most obvious. Of the nine allegations of neglect investigated with a parental interview, six concerned incidents of children being left unsupervised, and three were concerned with more general neglect related to mothers' alcohol consumption, two of which also involved inadequate supervision. Without exception, all the families concerned were experiencing a variety of other problems, including marital disharmony, housing difficulties, problems associated with addiction, chronic illness and depression. The investigative interviews, however, concentrated on the specific incident that led to the concern. In five out of the nine investigations, social workers recommended no further action, even though in three of them, 'neglect' was established, and in the other two, it was not disproved. The four cases where further interventions were recommended, and were allocated, included the three where the mothers' drinking caused significant and visible difficulties, and one that had a history of poor quality care and supervision.

While investigations of child sexual abuse may not universally be as clear-cut as they appear to be in this study, it does appear that it is in the areas of physical abuse and particularly neglect that social workers are forced to make more difficult decisions, replicating the findings of Gibbons *et al.* (1995) and Thorpe (1994). These were the situations that gave rise to most uncertainty and ambivalence, and this becomes more obvious when the criteria for assessment are examined.

Social workers were frequently non-specific about the sort of criteria which they employed to make assessments, but very often explained them in terms of the final disposal, employing what Thorpe (1994) and Parton *et al.* (1997) would term 'situated moral reasoning', which determined whether further action was required. If they decided, for example, to terminate the investigation, they tended to justify this in terms of certain impressions they had formed. As I have suggested, these were normally associated with the event that had provoked the referral in the first place, and acted to mitigate it, or confirm its gravity. The following areas appeared to have been the focus of social work attention.

With regard to the incident itself:

- strength of the evidence that abuse of some sort had occurred, although, as will be shown, 'substantiation' of the allegation did not necessarily lead to further intervention with the family.

In relation to the attitude and presentation of the parent or parents:

- parent/s' denial or affirmation of their responsibility
- parent/s' concern for the children and their understanding of what had happened
- strength of parent/s' ability to protect their children from further harm or risk
- mother's acknowledgement that harm had been inflicted on her child by someone else
- mother's appearance, and intelligence
- co-operation and openness of mothers.

When children were seen, the following factors were considered:

- disclosure of abuse from a child
- the relationship between child or children and parents, as observed during the investigative interview
- the attitude of the child to the social worker
- aspects of a child's condition, including physical welfare, mental health, and vulnerability, though these were rarely scrutinised to any degree.

Assessments were based on information gleaned from the above factors. Factors external to the interview, but which featured in a small number of instances, were comprised of:

- previous history of abuse by either parent
- previous history of the child being in care
- supports available to the mother
- the material circumstances of the family.

Some examples, first, of investigations that were concluded with a 'no further action' recommendation, will illustrate the above observations. In one instance, a lone female parent was reported for leaving her four-year-old daughter and her nine-year-old son unsupervised in her house one night. When the social worker visited, the mother was very contrite; in the words of the social worker she 'reiterated that she understood it was a wrong thing to do...she hadn't really thought it through and that it wouldn't happen again...' She spoke about her marital problems, and the fact that she was a recovering addict, using these facts as a justification for her need to 'get out'. Even though the social worker did not believe this was the first time the children had been left alone, he felt she had:

> ...been given a warning...I don't think the kids are at any particular danger, they look well enough, they look grand...I mean, I just don't think there's any cause for any future involvement, that would usefully be...what's the point in monitoring this?

Here, the judgement had been made on a quick appraisal of the house, the appearance of the children, and the mother's co-operative and 'correct' attitude, which validated her 'maternal identity' (Parton *et al.* 1997). This woman had initially been asked to call to the social work office during her break. She had telephoned to ask if, instead, the social worker could call to her after work. If she had actually come to the office, it is unlikely the children would have been with her and so their appearance would not have formed any part of the assessment. The main purpose of the interview was clearly to give her a 'warning', and observe her reaction. As the social worker acknowledged:

> It's a bit about the physical circumstances and about having seen the children, but it's not just that, it's about the fact that... I mean our ability to do anything else other than tell her it's wrong first off, and leave her with it. I mean, she is saying the appropriate things, whether I believe her or not, I mean, you have to take people...

In many ways, he was describing a type of ritual performance that was very focused on the misdemeanour committed by the mother in leaving her children unattended, measured against the appropriateness of her reaction to the social worker. The reasoning applied conformed to what Parton *et al.* (1997, p.87) describe as 'the way in which social workers articulated expectable features of parenting and utilised them in their judgements of child abuse claims'. As will be demonstrated, this was fairly typical assessment practice, one that focused far more on parental behaviour than on the extent to which children's needs were being met or not.

In another situation, a single mother in her thirties had been reported by her former babysitter for physically abusing her child and for 'coming home drunk late every night'. When the investigating social worker had interviewed her he was satisfied that no further action was needed. She had said, 'I do hit him [her son], I do smack him, and so what, all children get smacked and I'm not making any apologies for that'. She had denied the allegation that she came in drunk every night, and pointed out that the fact that she had recently had a row with the babysitter had probably prompted her to contact social services out of vengeance. Like the lone parent in the last example, this mother spoke about different stresses in her life, the burden of parenting alone, her inadequate accommodation, her lack of family support. Like the worker investigating the previous allegation, this social worker formed his judgement from his fairly short one-off meeting with the mother. He had spoken to her son briefly, to explain the purpose of his visit, and the child had responded to him but the social worker had formed no particular impression of him. The mother was not actually 'contrite', but her overall direct, and apparently honest, presentation reassured the worker sufficiently that her child was not at risk.

However, he was not entirely unequivocal about the worth of his investigation, as he pointed out:

> I don't know… I mean if I was genuinely trying to find out if she had abused or was potentially abusing her son physically, I would have had to have been much tougher, in terms of the questioning and much more abrasive, and I don't think that's possible, you know what I mean, I don't think we're able to do that…in these sort of situations, where the information is that unclear, I don't think we can assume guilt, or even…and I think you would have to assume guilt if you are going to do that sort of questioning… I don't think it arises in situations where somebody is saying a child has a very serious burn, or a child has a very serious black eye or something, in a situation like that you can be more abrasive about the questioning and I think people understand, but in a situation like this, it's nebulous, you don't really know where it's coming from or what the foundation of it is, or you can't go out and treat people in a more abrasive fashion really, you have to seek their co-operation as well.

Wise (1989), referring to the 'official knowledge' about child abuse that is presumed in child abuse inquiries, points to the assumption that child abuse is obvious and that only ineptitude prevents the adoption of a clear solution. The investigation just described offers an example of the ambiguity that surrounds many reports. As the social worker told the team meeting: 'All the allegations could be true, she's denying them, I don't know where that leaves us'. Parton *et al.* (1997, p.224) allude to the problematic nature of 'substantiation' where child abuse is concerned. They point out that in child abuse work, a substantiated case is not one that is subjected to legal standards of proof, but one where practitioners believe something may have occurred. The construction of abuse, or by inference, the *un*substantiation of abuse, occurs where one version of events is preferred over another, a process that cannot be separated from the wider social and political framework in which the response is made. The last two examples have illustrated the problematic nature of that process, as will the following two.

Another investigation that was carried out in response to a neglect allegation concerned a traveller family. The father had been approached by the police late at night when he was out begging with his three-year-old daughter. When he saw the police approaching him the father, according to the police report, 'abandoned the child in the street and drove away in a van'. The police subsequently placed the child with her extended family. This study has already demonstrated the statutory social workers' reluctance to intervene with the travellers. However, on this occasion, the abandonment of the child had breached the 'rule of optimism' (Dingwall *et al.* 1983), leaving the duty social worker no option but to carry out a home visit to the campsite. Having initially ascertained from other agencies involved that the children in this family were regarded as 'vulnerable', the social worker described her initial approach as follows:

> Well I was torn between trying to put this piece of behaviour that was causing concern…trying to put that in a cultural context and trying to work out whether it was going to be of any benefit to the family…to go out there and just give them the hard word really… I suppose what I was there to do really was… I wanted to see the child and the mother and to say to the mother that what had happened last night was unacceptable and that I wanted a guarantee from her that it wouldn't happen again, and that was really all I wanted to see. I mean I didn't even really want to see the child particularly, if the child had been down with other relatives or

> whatever, I wouldn't have asked for the child, I just wanted to see the mother...obviously she said when he (the father) left with the child he was going out to pick up some scrap and that she didn't know he was going drinking...she said he had taken the pledge, but I didn't believe any of that... I mean she *would* say it would never happen again.

The social worker had, as she suggested, fulfilled the 'letter of the law' by her visit, and the mother's guarantee of protection for her child. She was dubious, however, about the value of her assessment:

> Well, my assessment was...the child had no bruises as far as I could see...all the children were tumbling and playing together on this couch. I wasn't happy with the way the five-year-old was holding the baby...there was a gas fire between us and it wasn't lit, the child's head was very near the corner of this thing but it would have been hard to say whether the mother in a different situation would do something about that, she was very worried about what was going to happen to the children and what was going to happen to the husband, so it was hard to make an assessment... I felt my assessment wasn't worth anything.

In fact, despite the concentration of the interview on the incident where the child had been abandoned, the social worker felt that its seriousness had been exaggerated:

> The story was that he left the child and ran off, jumped into the van and ran off, but...he came back to the Gardaí and looked for the child, so I think that took some guts to do, you know... I think we're just reacting to something, like we're looking at it from our middle class views, on what's good enough child care and I don't think it's as bad as it sounds...what bothers me about it is that nothing is going to happen because all the agencies are just saying, 'Oh it's your job, it's your job, it's not our job'...

Another allegation, which will be discussed again later in some detail, concerned a family, reported by a neighbour, who claimed that the mother had been in the habit of leaving her children, aged two years, and six months, alone in the house while they were taking naps. The referrer also claimed that the mother was inclined to hit out and shout at the children. Preliminary telephone calls to her public health nurse and general practitioner established that this woman had a history of depression, and that one of the children previously had a health problem. The health problem was not life threatening but caused the child certain feeding difficulties as well as irritability. The children's father worked long hours and was able to contribute little in a practical way to their care. Unusually, a case conference was called before the parents were seen, and endorsed the need for an investigative interview. (This was the case previously mentioned where the father was asked to attend the interview with the mother to enable her to 'hear' what was being said.)

When the social worker met the parents in the office, they had the children with them. This had not been requested, but it gave the social worker an unexpected opportunity to see them. The parents were very upset at having been reported to social services; they denied that the children were ever left alone, or that they were physically or emotionally abused. They talked quite openly about their problems and said how hard they sometimes found it to cope. On the basis of a 30-minute interview, with no firm evidence beyond a denial that the neighbour's allegations had foundation, the social worker concluded that there was no need for further action. He based his assessment on:

> ...the way they presented as a couple really, the way they supported each other, the way the children presented, the way they were not saying 'Don't be ridiculous, we are the best parents in the world'; what they were saying is 'This is extremely hard, parenting is very difficult, you know and we have problems and we don't mind people's advice if you want to give us advice or whatever about that...we do our best for our children, they're not neglected and they're not mistreated'...they're open, I generally think their level of care is grand and that we let far bigger concerns go and we don't intervene, far far bigger concerns than these.

What these four investigations shared was a strong focus on the event that led to the report and a decision made, not on the substantiation or otherwise of that event, but on an understanding that the families had been 'warned'. Other than that, their assessments were made on a very impressionistic basis, with a heavy emphasis on the co-operative attitude of the parents that seemed to guarantee that the 'warning' had been taken. As the social worker who investigated the traveller family pointed out, 'the letter of the law' had been fulfilled. Altogether, 14 out of the 28 investigations concluded that no further action was needed. Figure 3.1 summarises the factors that were common to these conclusions.

- Lack of medical evidence of abuse
- Denial of the alleged event or concern
- A fuller, less daunting picture of the family with the incident placed in context
- Suspect motive on behalf of person making the referral
- Children's satisfactory physical appearance
- Children's satisfactory relationship with their parents, as observed during the interview
- 'General impression' (favourable) of mother
- Mother's appearance
- Mother's attitude to social worker
- Good material circumstances

Figure 3.1 Factors which appeared to lessen the gravity of the alleged incident or validate the allegation

Assessments which led to a recommendation for further intervention

The seriousness with which outcomes of assessment were regarded could be measured by the actions that followed, such as removal of a child to care, a decision to hold a case conference, or the allocation of a case to a social worker or other agency for continuing work. Fourteen of the twenty-eight child abuse referrals which were investigated by a parental interview were allocated to social workers for ongoing work, on the basis of concerns which are illustrated in Figure 3.2.

- 'Unfinished business' regarding child sexual abuse, including the need for validation and/or treatment
- Evidence and admission of physical abuse to child
- Depressed condition of child
- Sexual vulnerability of child
- Mother's alcoholism as a cause of neglect
- History of child having been in care combined with current concern about neglect
- Placement breakdown accompanied by evidence of physical abuse
- Evidence of children being left unsupervised (by their mother) on a continuous basis
- Age-inappropriate expectations of children by mother
- Mother's inability to appropriately discipline child
- Mother's continuing relationship with a violent partner

Figure 3.2 Child protection assessments which led to recommendations for further action

Analytically, the factors set out in Figure 3.2, several of which applied to some individual situations, could be divided into three categories of 'risk': particular incidents of abuse which were judged to be serious, judgements about mothers' parenting abilities, and factors to do with the vulnerabilities of the children themselves. Generally however, active responses to these or similar factors were not consistently made, as several of the above concerns were expressed with equal gravity with regard to situations that received no further follow up. In certain cases, the same risk factors were identified, but apparently *mitigated* for the following reasons, summarised in Figure 3.3.

- Co-operation of parents
- Openness to allegations and willingness to discuss them
- Honesty about parenting difficulties
- Indication by parent or parents of respect for authoritative intervention
- Appropriate contrition and promises not to repeat abusive incident
- Mothers' ability to get support from relatives
- Mothers' belief that abuse had occurred
- Acknowledgement that parent/s are doing their best in adverse circumstances

Figure 3.3 Mitigating circumstances which precluded further action by the child protection system in situations where recognised risk factors existed

The cases which were eventually allocated for further intervention lacked the mitigating features outlined above, most notably in relation to mothers' protective capacities which incorporate acknowledgement of the seriousness of the concern, contrition and levels of co-operation. When the individual cases are examined, this becomes clearer.

One of the sexual abuse cases, the M case detailed in the previous chapter, was particularly complex, and while the children were deemed to be protected by their mother immediately after the initial investigation, it was agreed that she would need ongoing support and that validation of the abuse and treatment of its aftermath would need to be co-ordinated. There was also the possibility of a police investigation. Two other sexual abuse cases were judged to need further action. One concerned a 13-year-old that had acknowledged sexually abusing his niece and the other involved a four-year-old who was allegedly abused by a babysitter. The purpose of intervention was the co-ordination of validation and treatment. Another investigation carried out on a sexual abuse case concluded that the by now very depressed victim, a teenage boy, should move out of home due to serious friction culminating in physical assault between himself and his mother – a case where maternal ability to protect had broken down, and 'maternal identity' (Parton *et al.* 1997) did not measure up to the required norm.

Certain investigations were carried out in the context of a 'crisis'; in these cases the critical events usually dominated the way the process unfolded. For example, a lone mother and her child were brought to hospital by the police following a fracas on the street between the mother and her ex-partner, the child's father. This family had already been referred to the Health Board because of an injury to the child caused by his father in the context of a violent assault on his mother, which culminated in his admission to hospital. The duty social worker in the Health Board had requested that the hospital social worker carry out an assessment at the time of the first admission. This had been done, and as the mother claimed she had left her violent partner, there appeared to be no ongoing concerns and no further action was taken by the Health Board social workers. Immediately following the new crisis and the second referral, reception of the child into care was considered by the Health Board social workers. The mother's co-operative attitude and contrition mitigated against that happening, but her 'history' of recidivism in relation to staying in contact with her violent ex-partner tended to undermine the trust the social workers were prepared to grant her, so her case was allocated for further interventions geared towards addressing her alcohol consumption and her relationship with her child's father.

Another situation, already briefly mentioned, where statutory social workers became involved in the midst of a crisis and carried out the investigation under pressure involved a seven-year-old boy who was allegedly physically assaulted by his adoptive mother, who claimed that she could not control his challenging behaviour. She asserted that she could not be responsible for her actions if the child was not removed into care immediately. The assessment of facts in this case left little choice other than to respond to the mother's threats by placing the child with a foster family.

Two other investigations into situations where maternal drinking was deemed to be a strong contributory factor in the neglect of children concluded that further action was necessary. These judgements were made in different contexts. In one, there was a history of repeated 'defaulting' by the mother, whose son had already spent two years in care. These facts contributed to pessimism about her rehabilitative potential. In the other situation, the children, most of whom were in their teens, virtually refused to accept the bleak and dangerous situation in which they were living any longer. They were constantly humiliated and embarrassed by their mother's behaviour when drunk, they had no money for food, and there was an ongoing risk that the mother might set fire to the house. Their father lived with them, but his protective capacity appeared very ineffective, and it was suspected that he too had a drink problem. In each of these cases, other professionals had become involved, in the first, the police and in the second, a school counsellor. A different investigation, concerning a lone parent who consistently left her four young children unsupervised, also actively involved police and a public health nurse. The neglect of the children was so blatantly in breach of the law, and the mother's attitude so unco-operative, that intervention was regarded as inevitable.

A unifying trend visible in all these cases is, once again, the flawed nature of the maternal identities, but these examples illustrate a number of other common factors in 'negative' assessments. The factors include not only failure of maternal protection and lack of co-operation, but a high degree of physical dangerousness and visibility about the child care concerns, and the pressure of other agencies' involvement. In many respects, the findings here suggest that it was only when it became unavoidable that interventions were made, and even when they went as far as investigating the allegations with parents, the pattern identified in the previous chapter was maintained, whereby social workers continued to exercise the 'rule of optimism'[1] conceived by Dingwall et al. (1983). In keeping with this theory, the 'rule' was breached in situations where parents failed to co-operate either in terms of their attitude, or their history of non-compliance with social work intervention (parental incorrigibility) and where other professionals were involved (failure of agency containment). As this chapter has demonstrated, the vast majority of referrals to the statutory social work service which were initially classified as 'child abuse/neglect' were discounted after investigation.

Fourteen of the allegations investigated by the statutory social workers were 'substantiated' to the point of further intervention, and as later chapters will show, three more were kept open by non-statutory agencies, who maintained a (non-specific) child protection 'brief' in their work with them. The potential for referrals to be screened out of the child protection system has been particularly highlighted in empirical research by Thorpe (1994) and Gibbons *et al.* (1995), and also by Parton *et al.* (1997), Buckley *et al.* (1997), Horwath (2001) and Buckley (2002). These studies infer that the narrow focus of the child protection 'culture' that operates in Australia, England and Ireland tends to consistently exclude situations that do not conform to particular norms of child abuse. The nature, for example, of neglect does not lend itself to easy classification and the contextual association of many child care problems with issues of poverty, ill-health, and other marginalising situations tends to blur boundaries between 'abuse' and other social stresses. The system, however, focuses more or less exclusively on evidence and not generalised deprivation or misery. In Ireland, child protection practice is not governed by procedural guidance to the same degree as it is in other countries, particularly the UK yet, as this study indicates, the same trend is visible.

It is interesting to note that many of the families featuring in this study, particularly those investigated for neglect, were experiencing other adversities which must have impacted to some degree on their children's welfare. Yet, it was solely the act which led to the referral that seemed to actually cross the threshold into 'abuse', for example, what appeared like isolated incidents where children were left unsupervised or were slapped or threatened in public. Stressors like poor mental or physical health, inadequate accommodation arrangements or addiction and marital or emotional problems were not, apparently, deemed to pose the same risk or danger. For example, a family with two young children were referred to 'duty' early in the fieldwork period, because of the mother's suspicions that the children were being sexually abused by their father. When the duty social worker interviewed the mother, he considered that her fears were groundless, as she had no evidence to support her suspicions. The social worker considered that the family had other serious problems, to do with housing, marital disharmony and 'the need for support'. He felt that some input into this family's situation 'would take hopefully a short period of time but...would make a huge difference to these children's lives'. In his view the mother 'had presented as an extremely distressed woman…under a lot of pressure and in bad need of accommodation'. However, when the referral was discussed at the team meeting, it was agreed that there were no grounds for any further investigation of sexual abuse, and closure was suggested. The social worker who had met the mother didn't agree with this decision, and protested:

> No… I'm concerned that this woman is extremely distressed, I would be concerned of her ability to cope with these two kids in the situation that she's in, and I think that she needs to be followed…we need to facilitate her getting accommodation. I think we need to facilitate her in that… I think the well-being of these two kids in this situation…they have been living in a squat…for a small amount of effort we can actually make a big difference.

The social worker described the potential for intervention in terms of 'a good piece of social work that we don't often get a chance to do in terms of all the other stuff that takes precedence'. But a colleague responded:

> But listen, we don't get involved with people about their housing no matter how distressed they are. I mean I have gangs of people in here terribly distressed about their housing circumstances, and that's not a priority… I've had people in here in floods of tears very distressed saying that their life is falling apart…we don't get involved in those situations…we're getting confused here I think, because there's an allegation of abuse being made here, and there appears to be no substance to that, there's certainly nothing that backs it up, the woman has problems, she's had problems for an awful long time, I just don't see it as a priority, I don't see why we would have any involvement with this woman given the other cases we have, we don't have time.

In the event, the investigation was terminated without further intervention at that time. Four months later, the mother re-referred herself to the service offering a more credible allegation that her husband was sexually abusing the children. At this point it was quickly allocated as a case of child sexual abuse. Shortly afterwards, the mother acknowledged that her allegations of sexual abuse were false, but the social worker stayed involved this time and made attempts to intervene in relation to the family's other needs. It is possible to speculate that even the mother in this situation realised that if she wanted to get a social worker to help her and her children with their problems, she had to frame her request in 'child abuse' terms. This pattern of focusing on specific issues re-appeared in a later Irish study on child neglect, which noted the tendency for statutory intervention to focus on individual events rather than applying a holistic approach (Horwath 2001).

The perceived value of orthodox child protection interventions

My assertion that the system was focused in such a narrow fashion as to exclude any factor outside the child abuse norm is not based exclusively on the above discussion of the way in which allegations were processed. It was also, as the next section will show, based on a 'sense' which became discernible through the voices of the practitioners themselves in relation to the value of their work, of which, they were on many occasions, quite sceptical. It must be acknowledged that the implementation of more formalised family support programmes in recent years may now mean that a different approach could be made. However, in the context of increased referral rates and staff shortages, traditional gate-keeping methods are still likely to apply, and it could be argued that many of the same norms operate as far as social work responses are concerned.

In this study it was clear that the concerns of workers centred principally on both the *purpose* and the *focus* of investigations, and were comprised of a number of elements. These included the social workers' unease with the application of a narrow measure of 'fitness to parent' within a context of other adversities over which they had little control; the impossibility of discriminating between 'abuse' and 'normal' parenting activity and the pointlessness of carrying out an investigation that achieves little and leaves parents feeling undermined and angry.

The practice of applying the 'letter of the law' as one worker had described it, to the exclusion of a full assessment of the family's situation, was critically highlighted by a worker who had investigated a 'neglect' referral. The parents in this instance were both drug users. They were in serious debt, were anxious to start treatment and had already been waiting six months to get on a methadone programme. They had been reported by a member of the public who had called to their house late one night and found the children on their own. The mother later described the circumstances surrounding that event to the investigating social worker, explaining that both she and her husband had been working. She expressed appropriate contrition, and said she had not considered the potential harm to the children. No further action was recommended. However, reflecting on this later, the social worker commented on the narrowness of the organisational perspective commonly applied to these types of situation:

> …my feeling is that what we were concerned about was not whether the children were in some unhappy or distressing, or vulnerable situation, but simply that we had information and an allegation, and to cover our own backs we needed to follow that and clear it out of the way and that's what the focus, I think, is…it was simply a matter of following through a procedure about an allegation in order that the agency covers itself…

The actual response had, according to this practitioner, little to do with the context in which the alleged neglect of the children was taking place, the drug use, the lack of money and the tensions experienced by the parents in waiting for a methadone programme. The object of professional attention was the act of leaving the children alone for two hours:

> …we're following a pattern…you need to go out and tell them not to do it…they say yes I'll never do it again and we say fine… We've done our bit, you know what I mean…that's what it feels like to me…

The sense of frustration experienced by this practitioner reflects Thorpe's (1994, p.202) theory that child protection investigation and assessment may, by their failure to acknowledge the social context within which concerns arise, have only a tenuous link with 'protection', focusing more on the moral behaviour of parents, and enforcing 'standard middle-class patriarchal child rearing norms'. That notion was reinforced in this study by the seeming impossibility of setting boundaries around adequate and inadequate care. Apart from the difficulty of agreeing on 'reasonable' standards, social workers, as this chapter has already demonstrated, felt that the expectation that they could actually discern whether or not 'abuse' had been committed was invidious:

> …I mean, you are going out on all these nebulous things that can't be resolved one way or another, you go out and somebody tells you something…how can you possibly know whether you believe them or not? And then somebody says to you, this is where the professional judgement

supposedly comes in, and this is a game as well…what is your professional judgement? Do you think the children are at risk? How are you supposed to know? You couldn't possibly know, you don't know. This is what the person said, and that's all we know…impossible things being expected…

Another social worker made a similar comment

…even the whole thing of what is true and what is not true, even that's a philosophical dilemma! Some people say: 'It did happen, but let me explain the context, and when you hear the context it didn't'… It's neither right nor wrong in the context, so it's not as simple as it's A or B or black or white… It is more complicated when you are actually out there…

A worker who had followed up an allegation of physical abuse but was able to reach no firm conclusion reiterated his frustration about the organisational framework, which in his view applied a very narrow focus on child care concerns:

I think the organisation would be happy because we went out, we got the information…it had to be checked out, this had to be done, I mean…all I have done is give people a lot of generalised information, nobody is asking any questions, I mean are people satisfied that this is ok? Do we now close this? But what have we gained? Why is nobody asking any questions? …I'm the one who did the assessment and I have said that I have absolutely no idea whether these allegations are true or not, I mean how do we make a decision to close it? We're in no better position than we were last week.

The allegation made against the mother who was accused of leaving her children while she went out was outlined earlier. When the social worker spoke to me after his interview, he felt his intervention had actually made the situation worse for the family:

…my assessment is that we've really messed these people's lives up badly…they've got an extremely hard time… She suffered from post-natal depression… They as a family went through a very difficult time and now they have this allegation…and subsequently to this interview she rang me back and sounded completely…you know, completely lost her head over the whole thing…

Another worker made a similar point regarding a different investigation and referred to the pointlessness of intervening with a child abuse investigation when the problems being experienced by the family were linked with much broader issues:

> ...the problem about going out to visit people...the devastation you leave... That's one of the big things...if you are going out and it's just a matter of people being questioned about their child care practices, and then you walk away and everything is ok, but we know that everything is not ok, and that we have nothing to offer... We're coming from an agency that's supposed to be talking about child welfare aren't we? And all we can do is go out and do this to people... It's giving a very double message.

The notion that child protection work could be done in a manner that was more sensitive, involving partnership or in a manner which would engage clients on a more egalitarian level, was dismissed out of hand:

> Our job is not to go out there and co-operate with parents...they're not going to say to you 'Yes I do this and I do that'... They're going to think of all sorts of convoluted excuses as to why the child has bruises or why they're masturbating in the classroom or whatever, and somehow we have got to go beyond that, so we're not dealing in a situation where we go out and say 'I want to help you'... People come knocking on the door saying... 'You are considered by somebody and now you are an officially designated child abuser', and that's the hidden message, I don't care how nice we are about it... We underestimate, I think, the power of that.

Parton *et al.* (1997) talk about the impossibility of modifying the 'thresholds' which determine whether or not to apply a 'family support' or 'child protection' approach within a political framework which seeks to eliminate risk and still requires workers to prioritise their work within limited resource provision. Similar issues were debated by the social workers in this study, who felt caught between the public perception attached to their role, and the reality of day-to-day practice. As the previous chapter has indicated, practitioners felt that their work was being driven by what they described as 'politicians and the media' who, as one of the social workers put it, base 'their expectations around a lack of understanding of the complexity of it, or understanding of how these things impact on families'.

The UK child protection research overview (Department of Health 1995) suggests a switch in focus from investigation to assessment of 'need'; this issue has been debated by Parton *et al.* (1997) and Parton and Mathews (2001) who find the notion of such a change in perspective quite problematic, partly because of the trend in recent years to cut back, rather than expand on service provision. Similarly, the workers in this study were sceptical about the employment of 'resources' as an adequate solution to their current dilemma. In relation to a suggestion that more parenting courses should be introduced, for example, one worker responded:

> Most of them don't want that... I knew a woman who kept choosing courses that she knew didn't exist so that she wouldn't ever have to actually do them... You see, of course there should be a lot more resources like that but the people who are motivated will pick them up anyway, they don't need a social worker to come out and complain to get them to do it... The ones we tend to get involved with are so devastated by their own lives and their background that they are not organised enough, that's the problem, to get themselves to these places. They are the ones I'd be most worried about.

This worker had a fairly radical alternative approach in mind:

> I think if we stopped being so intrusive, if we didn't take on this huge responsibility that we seem to take on and we didn't allow it to be imposed upon ourselves... I don't think there would be many children abused who are not going to be abused anyway, and it would cost the taxpayer a lot less money... If we could concentrate on situations where there is substantial abuse, clearly those children need to be taken out of those situations, some intervention is necessary and that's a very purpose-ful, valuable thing to be doing and I'm not for a minute saying that social work is hopeless and ineffective... I think what happens though, is that we try to become involved in so many situations that we can do nothing about, that we feel ineffective... If we could confine ourselves to the things that need to be done...or a situation where people are asking for help, they are the two situations where I think we can be effective, or we can do good work. All the other stuff...

This worker was, despite his obvious sincerity in critiquing current approaches to work, minimising the dilemmas involved in deciding which were the most serious cases and excluding the others. This point was debated by Parton *et al.* (1997), who point out that if we accept that child abuse is a socially constructed phenomenon, then it is not a simple matter to discriminate between the 'serious' and 'less serious' cases. Nevertheless, the last section illustrates the gulf that the social workers perceived to exist between the reality of day-to-day practice and the discourse which they consider has developed in relation to child protection. As the previous chapter also demonstrated, despite the considerable discretion they allow themselves in relation to responding to reported concerns about children, the social workers clearly feel constrained by the system. They visualise themselves as operating, when they do intervene, within a narrow, forensic framework; as one of the social workers quoted above put it, 'simply…following through a procedure about an allegation in order that the agency covers itself'. They were clearly expressing disillusionment with the 'service' they were providing, which they believed a lot of the time to be inadequate, misdirected and potentially destructive.

Conclusion

As the last two chapters have shown, much of the work in child protection is comprised of the activities of screening and filtering, which are directed at assessing risk to children but are complicated by competing motives such as the desire to avoid unwarranted intrusions into people's lives in situations where little could be achieved by their interventions, the necessity to keep caseloads manageable, and a determination to share the responsibility for the 'dirty work' of child protection with other professionals. As the practice has been described, it becomes clear that responses to 'child abuse' allegations do not conform to the relatively straightforward framework outlined in the child protection guidelines. Rather the work is shaped by the 'sense-making' activities of the child protection practitioners.

As a result, decisions regarding children's potential safety or otherwise appear to be reached through a process of negotiation, where impressionistic assessments, or what Thorpe (1994) and Parton *et al.* (1997) term 'situated moral reasoning' is applied to each situation as it arises. Such judgements are, by the practitioners' own admission, frequently prone to error. As two of the social workers describe it, they were often left feeling they couldn't either 'control' or 'get a handle on what is expected'. An aspiration to alter their practice was expressed, whereby they would be required only to deal with the most serious situations where children were being harmed. Yet, the workers themselves were dubious that the system could incorporate this type of radical change. As one practitioner pointed out, what would be required would be 'changing our job description'. This dilemma is emphasised by Parton *et al.* (1997), who argue that within the current climate, where so many referrals are made in the form of allegations, re-labelling or re-defining allegations before they are investigated would be very difficult. Although such a practice actually operated in Ballyowen, the social workers clearly did not either realise the degree to which they employed so much flexibility, or feel that they could adopt it openly as a strategy for responding to reports.

In this study, the social workers' discomfort with the direction that their professional role had adopted appeared to justify the considerable latitude they exercised in their investigative work, whereby they tended to give the parent/s the benefit of the doubt unless they were compelled to act otherwise. These judgements were carried out within what Dingwall *et al.* (1983) term the 'liberal compromise', which dictates the limits of intrusion into family privacy beyond which workers are reluctant to go.

As this chapter has shown, a quarter of the original allegations survived the initial filtering processes and received some form of intervention. This number included three cases which had been referred twice for child abuse concerns, but which were closed without further action on the first occasion. Given the invisible nature of much child maltreatment, it is not possible to definitively claim that all the judgements made in relation to the closed referrals were correct; the chances are that, in some cases, children had in fact been 'abused' or harmed and continued to be after the investigation was terminated. However, one could speculate, on the basis that so few situations reappeared in the statistics, that the majority of decisions to close with no further action were the appropriate ones, within the 'brief' operated by the social workers.

As this chapter has made clear, whatever their dissatisfactions or frustrations about failing to address the broader adversities experienced by families, the practitioners considered their official remit to be the investigation of 'abuse' within the framework that they had constructed for assessing it, which did not include welfare concerns. To that extent, their practice met the required standards, or so it would seem. Yet, as has been demonstrated, the activity they practised was largely based on what at times seemed like serendipitous and largely impressionistic sense-making, achieved in ways which would be unlikely to stand up well to any scrutiny measured in relation to official procedures. The failure to address either contextual issues, or interactional processes such as those identified by Reder *et al.* (1993) and Reder and Duncan (1998), may fit within the requirements of the child protection discourse, but means that important aspects of child protection and welfare are excluded from assessment. These findings once again emphasise the crucial part played by method-ological paradigms such as the one taken in this book. Neither the social contexts in which child abuse reports are constructed, nor the reasoning applied by practitioners in responding to them, would be visible if a tech-nical rational approach, which pays no attention to the problematic nature of the process, was employed.

This chapter, and the previous one, have described and analysed the early responses to allegations of child abuse reported to the Ballyowen social work team by either professionals or members of the public. The process of assessment is, of course, continued throughout the careers of cases, and decisions are frequently evaluated and modified. The multi-disciplinary child protection conference provides a well-established, officially endorsed forum for discussion and review of child protection sit-uations. The next chapter will examine this aspect of the child protection machinery, and discuss the various processes which underpin its function-ing.

Endnote

1   Dingwall *et al.* (1983) define 'the rule of optimism' as a rule by which 'staff are required, if possible, to think the best of parents' (p.79). The rule, in their view, provides two 'institutional devices' by which most sources of concern can be discounted. These they named 'cultural relativism' and 'natural love'. Cultural relativism is explained as an 'agency justification', meaning that 'the ascription of deviance is correct, but that in practice, the observed conduct is permitted or required by the particular circumstances' (p.82). Under the rule,

members of one culture could not justifiably criticise members of another by employing their own normative standards.

The other device which may be used to neutralise, or re-frame deviance is, according to the authors, an 'excuse' which they call 'natural love'. Like justifications, excuses recognise deviance, but moral liability is withheld on the grounds of an impairment of the actor's capacity-responsibility. Justifications, say Dingwall *et al.*, can be seen in terms of a social framework, but excuses are situated 'in the realm of nature' (p.86). The assumption is that parents love their children 'as a fact of nature' (p.87), therefore they are not capable of hurting them.

Chapter Four

The Child Protection Conference

The child protection conference basically consists of an inter-disciplinary and inter-agency meeting, attended by a variety of professionals involved in a particular case. As objects of research, child protection conferences facilitate the observation of several aspects of child protection practice, particularly the way in which information is reported and processed, and the criteria that are applied to assessment and decision-making. Equally, they provide an ideal location for examination of the interactional processes which are fundamental to the much desired 'co-ordination' of child protection work, and which have been the subject of so much attention in child abuse inquiry reports (Reder *et al.* 1993; Reder and Duncan 1998). As a research approach, pluralistic evaluation (Smith and Cantley 1985) is also facilitated by the opportunity to include the involvement of different agents in the child protection network.

Whilst promoting the importance and necessity for conferences in child protection work, procedural guidelines tend to assume the willingness of practitioners and managers not only to attend, but also to co-operate with one another, offer mutual respect, and reach realistic and achievable decisions. Yet by their very nature child protection conferences are prone to a range of factors that strongly impact on their effectiveness. They are unique to the extent that they bring together a range of perspectives, which inevitably give rise to certain, though not always unhealthy, tensions. Mistaken beliefs about the worth of child protection conferences were identified by Reder *et al.* (1993) and earlier by Hallett and Stevenson (1980) whose analysis from over two decades ago still has pertinence for current practice. Both these works have offered the view that conferences can be the objects of unrealistically high expectations, given the complicated nature of the processes involved and the potential for rivalries, prejudices and stereotyping to come to the fore.

This chapter will illustrate some of these complexities and again emphasise the contrast between the idealised 'official' version of this element of child protection machinery and the reality of its operation in the social world of day-to-day practice. It must be said at the outset that the interview data relating to child protection conferences demonstrated, for the most part, favourable views as to their value in protecting children. This chapter, however, mainly focuses on dynamics that may not normally get much attention and yet impact, often negatively, on the potential for conferences to achieve their objectives.

The child protection conferences

Nine of the child abuse allegations from the core of this research led to the decision to hold an initial conference. Later during the fieldwork period, seven other inter-agency meetings were held to discuss four of the same families. These were termed 'review' conferences, their purpose being to update current information and review the adequacy of the initial decisions and plans. I observed 14 of the 16 child protection conferences, eight of which were initial meetings and six of which were reviews. The analysis of conferences described in this chapter is comprised of my own observations, but also reflects the perspectives of a range of participants. Interviewees included the senior area medical officer/acting Director, social work manager, statutory social workers, public health nurses, senior public health nurses, police, general practitioners, child psychiatrists, an adult psychiatrist, psychologists, therapists, counsellors and non-statutory social workers. The interviews concerned specific issues to do with the particular conference and also incorporated the participants' wider observations about the child protection system.

It became very clear through observation of the meetings, and interviews with the participants, that the less visible or acknowledged interactions and processes that operated at the conferences had a profound impact on the flow of the meeting, the decisions and the recommendations.

However, though many of the perspectives offered by the interviewees were extremely critical, pointing to deficiencies in the conferences themselves and the child protection system in general, the positive components of the meetings were consistently and frequently acknowledged. The majority of professionals who attended conferences considered them worthwhile despite their less useful aspects. Yet many of their judgements would have been conditional on the successful implementation of the plans proposed during the meetings, which did not always transpire.

Amongst the tasks which were perceived to have been accomplished by the case conference were cited the 'sharing of information', 'acknowledgement of children and families' problems', 'planning', and 'tying up loose ends'. They were seen as educative, informative and useful in 'planning a co-ordinated approach'. It is important to note that child protection conferences held under Irish child protection procedures differ in one important respect from those held in the UK: they are not intended to consider the matter of whether a child's name should be placed on the child protection register. As explained in Chapter Two, the information management system operated by the Irish health boards differs from that in other jurisdictions.

In examining the part played by child protection conferences in the child protection system, this chapter concentrates on the following factors:

- the purpose and function of the conference, including attendance

- the type and quality of information reported by different participants

- the nature of the discussion and development of the decision making process

- inter-agency and inter-professional issues

- conference plans, arrangements for carrying them out, and whether or not plans were considered feasible or realistic

- the way in which case conference decisions were conveyed to parents.

Not all child abuse allegations, even when they were substantiated and appeared serious, were the subjects of conferences. They were normally only convened when there was a need to plan intervention in a complex situation, such as the sexual abuse case described in the previous chapter, or where negotiations between agencies or professionals were required, and there was a need to pool knowledge and information. Apart from the Health Board, the agencies that most commonly participated in the conferences featuring in this study were treatment services including: the child and adult psychiatric services, addiction services, counselling services, child sexual abuse assessment services, treatment services for perpetrators and victims of child sexual abuse and the local women's refuge.

It must be pointed out here that full parental attendance at child protection conferences was not the norm at the time the fieldwork for this study was conducted. This obviously limits the value of the data and analysis in terms of the way that inter-professional dynamics are played out and managed in the presence of parents or carers. Nonetheless, the factors that could be illustrated are still of relevance to any consideration of inter-professional and inter-agency relationships as well as the management of meetings where information is exchanged, perspectives are constructed and decisions are made.

Purpose and function of child protection conferences

The reason for holding child protection conferences in Ballyowen was ostensibly to fulfil the need to share information, by means of, according to the social work manager, 'listening to the concerns of an outside agency and co-ordinating with the people on the ground'. The 'official' aims were, therefore, to discuss perspectives and make plans, with the welfare of the children involved as a priority. However, closer examination revealed that just under half of the meetings were called, not strictly to fulfil the stated aims, but principally to deal with undercurrents of inter- and intra-agency tension, where various professionals had been unable to reach consensus in a less formal setting. For example, it would be unusual to have a conference to discuss an initial allegation of neglect before investigating it, yet in one case it was held before the parents were contacted. On examination, it transpired that the decision to have a meeting in this instance was the result of an altercation between a public health nurse and the social work manager, who intended it to resolve the difficulty:

> The public health nurse took umbrage at something I had said to her …so I felt that in the light of these dynamics… I remembered that really we have often had case conferences…not just where a child has been notified but…on concerns, inter-agency communication…so I felt 'let's have one'…

In another case, a conference was convened because social workers from the Health Board and a non-statutory treatment service had been unable to reach consensus on the telephone about the need to co-ordinate an investigation. It became very obvious on these occasions that the children concerned took second place to the acting out of various agendas and rivalries, using the conference as a battlefield. This issue will be discussed more fully later in the chapter.

Apart from the usual Health Board personnel, the most frequent attendees at child protection conferences were police, who attended eight out of the fourteen meetings. The most frequently invited non-participants were general practitioners, who came to four out of the eleven they were asked to attend, in keeping with precedents identified in other studies (Hallett 1995; Farmer and Owen 1995; Polnay 2000). Teachers attended two of the three conferences they were invited to.

Five lone (female) parent families were the subjects of ten conferences, and in three of these cases, there was a male parent figure who lived elsewhere. In one of the families, the mother had a male cohabitee who acted in a paternal role. In another, the father was not living with the mother and child but had frequent, unplanned, contact. In a third, the father had left the family at the beginning of the investigation but had regular contact.

Information reported to child protection conferences

The child protection conferences normally followed a format of introductions, presentation of individual reports, discussion, and formulation of plans. Contributions tended to follow a pattern. The key worker in the agency requesting the meeting was normally asked to speak first, and would usually report on the following issues:

- agency contact with family
- family's social history
- mother's personality, attitude to children, ability to care emotionally and physically for the child or children
- family relationships, including child's relationship with parents
- details of recent event or incident
- agency response to the incident
- mother's ability to protect child
- parent's admission of guilt
- child's credibility when disclosing abuse
- parent/s' response to incident and to agency involvement
- parental co-operation
- previous work done with parent, usually mother, and previous concerns
- perception of immediate needs.

Other participants would be then asked to contribute their information, in whatever order the chairperson considered most appropriate. The public health nurse's contribution would contain information on the child's general development, particularly speech and language, the child's physical well-being, emotional development, behaviour and level of physical care. Additionally, the public health nurse would usually report on the mother's ability to meet her children's emotional needs, her relationship with them, and if relevant, mother's own emotional well-being or physical health. She would usually also comment on the appearance of the family home, any safety issues in the home, and any history of illness or hospitalisation of family members. Like social workers, public health nurses rarely commented on the involvement of fathers in those situations where they either lived with or had frequent contact with their children, a trend otherwise noted in research (Kingston 2001; Edwards 1998).

If a treatment or assessment agency were represented, their accounts would usually contain the following information:

- the parent/s' and child's engagement and co-operation with the agency
- personality of child
- birth history of child
- child's developmental progress
- child's educational progress
- child's emotional state
- family lifestyle
- presentation and personality of parents, including marital history
- mother's mental state
- mother's personality and intellectual capacity
- mother's capacity to parent.

It is notable that even where fathers lived with the families or had contact, the carer whose capacity to meet the child's need was judged by the treatment agencies was inevitably the mother. The general practitioners' contributions would be very similar to the assessment and treatment agencies, although they would normally refer to other siblings as well as the child under discussion. In some instances they had a more in-depth knowledge of the extended family and the pattern of relationships, having in two cases treated several generations of the one family.

On the two occasions where schools were represented, the reports from teachers outlined their impressions of the child's personality, his or her relationship with peers, school attendance patterns, educational progress and ability, health problems, and the mother's involvement with school. On each occasion, the teacher left before the end of the conference in order to get back to work, and in one case the teacher expressed the wish for the school to be 'out' of the situation because her principal was worried about the legal implications.

The fieldwork for this study was conducted just prior to the publication of guidelines (Department of Health 1995) that formalised Health Board relationships with An Garda Síochána. However, the involvement of the police in child protection work was becoming increasingly prevalent, following the recommendations of the Kilkenny Report (Department of Health 1993) and the presence of police at over half of the conferences bears witness to this. Generally, their contributions consisted of discussions about the feasibility or likelihood of a prosecution, the advisability of pressing charges, the encouragement of children to make statements, the verification of incidents that had been witnessed and the value of evidence from the police perspective. A lot of time was given to discussing procedural matters, such as timing of reporting, how investigations were generally processed by the police, and the limits as to how far they could become involved.

It is interesting, given the findings reported in the previous chapter, to note that reports by social workers, particularly those representing the Health Board, tended to prioritise the same sort of factors which underpinned the child protection investigations and assessments prior to the conference, that is, around the incident or concern itself. This would be combined with an account of the parents', usually the mother's, reaction to it and her general personality, co-operativeness and parenting capacities. Other professionals, in general, offered broader perspectives; for example, the public health nurses and teachers focused a lot more on the children, as did the general practitioners, linking their behaviour to expectations around the children's emotional and physical development and their social and familial context. These professionals also applied moral judgements about maternal 'attitudes', lifestyles and capacities but not as exclusively.

The ability of the conference to make accurate assessments inevitably depended on the type and quality of information presented. As the interview data demonstrated, this was frequently considered to be good where reports were detailed, succinct and comprehensive. The contributions, for example, from the child sexual abuse assessment unit were generally praised. However, in several instances, participants who were interviewed by me considered that information had been incomplete, negatively focused on the incident or concern which had precipitated the referral, poorly prepared, lacking in 'expert' opinion and frequently ignorant of wider contextual issues. It was also noticeable that material circumstances were rarely mentioned, and despite the fact that ten of the fourteen conferences concerned lone female parents, socio-economic or any other issues outside of individual moral characteristics and families' willingness to change, did not feature greatly in the accounts offered. Apart from a decision to support a housing application in one instance, services that were nominated did not include financial or material help. This pattern replicates findings of research in the UK (Farmer and Owen 1995; Thoburn *et al.* 1995) and a later Irish study focusing on professional responses to child neglect (Horwath 2001).

The nature of the discussion and development of the decision-making process

The conference discussions following the delivery of reports appeared to replicate the trend that had been visible in the initial assessments, dwelling more on recent events than on past history or the social context of the family. The meanings attached to recent concerns and their potential risk or seriousness were discussed, along with speculation about potential further abuse. Optional ways of assisting the family were usually suggested that may or may not have had direct relevance to the risk or concern discussed, but whose aims were generally to prevent its reoccurrence. Stevenson (1995), on the basis of research carried out in the UK, suggests that the assessment of risk tends to dominate child protection conferences at the expense of other welfare concerns. Even though the functions of conferences in the context of this study were less formally defined than they would be in Britain (Department of Health [UK] 1991, 1999), discussion at the conferences featuring in this study also tended to centre around the area of harm or potential risk to children, and it was on the basis of this tariff that resources were allocated and plans were made.

It was clear that agencies outside the statutory service framed their concerns in terms of child abuse risk, which they saw as a way of getting resources. However, there was less of a flavour of legalism in the case conferences featuring in this study. While the possibilities and feasibility of taking legal proceedings, both civil and criminal, were discussed at most of the meetings, the orientation appeared to be more in the direction of framing situations as 'deserving' in the moral sense and 'in need' in the practical sense, rather than as evidence for court. There was a definite reluctance, openly expressed, towards removing children from their families.

One significant theme that featured prominently in the conference discourse was the level of co-operation and integrity that could be expected from the parents, usually the mother. This was normally resolved via an exchange of views on her moral character and culpability for the incident which led to the abuse allegation, again following a very similar framework to that operated in the initial investigations carried out by the Health Board social workers. Responsibility and blame for the incident tended to rest with the parent who was now in charge, who was almost always the mother. For example, there were musings over whether or not one mother had 'turned a blind eye' to the fact that her husband was abusing the children. The fact that a mother who had been deemed neglectful 'wasn't interested' in help, and 'denying things' was central to the discussion in another case conference. The 'weak' character of a woman who was a victim of violent abuse from her partner, but who drank excessively ('turns on the tears very easily without much depth' and 'had promised the same things a hundred times before'), was central to the conference discussion about her capacity to parent.

The moralising tenor was occasionally carried into discussion about possible solutions, for example, whether a lone mother would make good use of the break that would be provided by offering respite care for her children, other than 'going out on Saturday night and having a good time'. It is debatable whether these considerations would have been so visible if the parent/s had been present, though there is some evidence from research that the actual presence of parents at child protection conferences can provide further scope for the adjudication of their characters, according to how they behave and react (Christie 1993; Thoburn *et al.* 1995; Corby, Millar and Young 1996; Bell 2000).

Child protection conferences lasted, on average, one and a half hours, though some could be as long as two hours, particularly if there were contentious inter-agency issues. The chairperson consciously attempted to keep them within a limited time-frame in order to prevent participants from getting, as she described it, 'bogged down'. The tendency for discussions to be curtailed by time constraints has already been highlighted by Farmer and Owen (1995) and their finding is replicated in this study, where there was evidence that participating professionals were irritated by the 'drive' towards reaching conclusions and making plans. Interviewees expressed frustration with the narrow focus of some of the meetings that prevented exploration of the conceptual aspects of the abuse situations themselves. There was a general view that discussion was dominated by the specific concern that had precipitated the conference, excluding the broader context, or any deeper examination of the nature of the 'abuse' itself, its aetiology, impact and prognosis for treatment or reoccurrence.

The lack of theoretical reasoning at the conferences in this study was noted by some social workers. For example, in an interview, the social work manager bemoaned the absence of any serious discussion about why a lone mother persistently left her children unsupervised and the failure of the conference to make any attempt to get to the root of the problem. In relation to another case of serious intra-familial abuse, one of the Health Board social workers suggested that there should have been more discussion on the type of dynamics that operated in sexually abusive families. However, when interviewed, the person who normally chaired the conferences, though acknowledging the educative benefits of such theoretical analysis, expressed her view that it would be 'indulgent' and distracting from the main purpose.

Some participants who were interviewed were concerned about the gulf between professional opinions that were expressed at the conferences and the 'reality' of clients' living situations. A police officer, for example, who was involved in investigating the continued neglect of children by their mother was a bit sceptical about the social workers' optimistic view of the situation:

> ...from my point of view I see the realities as I see them, and I tend to feel that the social workers...tend to give as best an account of [the mother] as they can, whereas I see the realities from day-to-day, from last year and the year before. I've seen her drunk, I've seen her picking up fellows in various situations...

Local authority social workers, according to Pithouse (1987, p.23), tend to see themselves used as a 'dustbin' for other agencies' problems, and deal with this by criticising and naming the shortcomings of other agencies, denying their validity. Criticisms, Pithouse claimed, are frequently based on the judgement that 'only those who really "know" what day-to-day work is all about can understand or comment on the occupational task'. Elements of this tendency were observable in the attitudes of statutory social workers in this study who, following child protection conferences, often voiced distrust of the therapies offered by the treatment agencies, seeing them as at a remove from families' everyday lives and reflecting not so much concern about parents or children as what one social worker described as 'professional appropriateness'. In line with this attitude, the strict operation of a paradigm (in one case the particular model of treatment for sex offenders by a treatment agency) was regarded with cynicism, being described as a 'rigid philosophy' that provides more safety for workers than effective change in a client. Some of the expectations expressed at the conferences by non-statutory staff were regarded by the social workers as 'pie in the sky' and unrealistic, for example, the recommendation that a family would be visited daily.

Inter-agency and inter-professional tensions

Reder *et al.* (1993) noted the tendency for professionals within the network to develop attitudes and beliefs about one another and their respective roles in cases. Their theory was illustrated in this study by the way that some participants brought their 'baggage' into the case conference with them. Participants in the research spoke of agencies 'being lined up' against each other, reflecting underlying conflicts and tensions that had been building up around cases during the previous weeks. It was acknowledged by some of them that inter-agency difficulties had tended to dominate the conferences at times, preventing the emergence of a clear view of the families and their situations. In some instances, it was suggested that most of the energy expended by professionals at the conferences went into what were described as 'political and professional considerations', centring on issues like responsibility for particular tasks. These processes had the effect, according to the chairperson, of impeding discussion with 'both sides stopping too short...people almost afraid to talk in case it means they have to do something'.

'Exaggeration of hierarchy' is identified by Reder *et al.* (1993) as a barrier to good communication between professionals and agencies. Likewise, Hallett and Stevenson (1980) recognised the perceived and sometimes mistakenly elevated status of some members as a significant influence on the way that information is heard. Examples of this tendency became visible at several points in this research. For example, a child psychiatrist at one child protection conference was not particularly disposed to value the contribution of the public health nurse who wanted a simple solution to the mother's child care problems. This consisted of involving the children's grandmother rather than bringing in a professional child care worker. In an interview after the conference, the psychiatrist observed:

> I think maybe the public health nurse didn't have an understanding of the [family] dynamics, which made others who would have understood the dynamics a bit irritated with her... I think it was just a lack of understanding, which I don't think she could be expected to have, to be honest!

The public health nurse herself was aware that her views were not accorded much credibility by the child psychiatric team:

> I think I was heard as a voice kind of complaining, I don't know if I was heard... I mean [the chairperson] listened to me, but I don't think it was perceived necessarily as a valuable contribution.

In the event, the recommendations of the child psychiatric service were endorsed by the conference over and above the public health nurse's suggestions. Ironically, they ultimately proved unworkable.

Another example of the operation of 'exaggerated hierarchy' was present at one of the review conferences concerning a family where sexual abuse had been disclosed. A psychologist who was treating one of the children and a therapist from a service that was treating the perpetrator, had strong opinions to offer, to the irritation of one of the statutory social workers:

> Everybody seemed to be hanging on [the psychologist's] every word, and in fact what she was saying wasn't very sensible, and the two things don't hang together... I find that very aggravating really, that if you have a

family support worker there who's saying very sensible things people don't pay attention because she has no status…whereas somebody like [the psychologist] can walk in and say daft things and everybody has to listen very carefully…

Doctors in primary practice, according to Dingwall (1980, p.118) claim a 'super ordinate' role, which is essentially determined by their 'training for personal responsibility and a sense of self confidence amounting to dogmatism', and the conference, he suggests is 'one of the more public arenas for accomplishing institutional subordination'. In this study, the tendency to give priority to doctors was noticed by a number of participants. Examples included the priority given to psychiatrists, even though they were members of a multi-disciplinary team who all had contributions to make. It was noted that the chairperson, who was a medical doctor, tended to shake hands with and introduce any participating doctors but not any other professionals, and for doctors to address each other exclusively during the meetings.

Members of the police attended eight child protection conferences. Despite their willingness to attend, they did not always feel welcome, and some of their reactions reflected the lack of trust that appeared to exist between themselves and the other agencies. A police officer at one conference said: 'I think there is a tendency at times to have the Garda personnel present, but its more to oversee, to say "Well, we had the Gardaí present". His view was shared by a female colleague at the same meeting: 'There was a whole power struggle going on…one of the social workers made some sly comment about [what] the family thought of the Gardaí…' She felt that this 'power struggle' interfered with the discussion 'because you're getting off the point, you're getting away from the victim and the family'. What she called 'boundaries between the doctors and the rest of us' impeded the police from getting what she might have considered important information.

Working together

Despite episodes of sharing and working together between some professionals and the importance attributed to joint work and co-operation, what could be described as lack of 'team spirit' operated at some child protection conferences. In fact, one of the unacknowledged functions of the conference seemed to be its facility to demonstrate how unco-ordinated workers could be in their activities. This became very clear to the social worker in a sexual abuse case, at a critical point when she reflected on her professional isolation and spoke about how she felt after a conference:

> It's strange…not as frustrated as coming out of previous case conferences because I felt that it was stated so clearly that there was no ambivalence any more about what I had been saying previously, and that is, 'Look, I'm here on my own'. And in a way that was a bit of a relief even though it was awful…even if the others were kind of pulling back and out and saying 'We don't want anything to do with it', it gave us…I thought, anyway, a new starting point to go off and maybe find others who would do the work that was necessary, or to examine our own resources to do the work.

At the same case conference, tensions appeared to run high between the social worker and a psychologist. As Reder *et al.* (1993, p.66) have observed, what they term 'dormant professional rivalries' and presentations of 'infallibility' may cause workers to lose sight of their primary functions and co-operation. One of the other participants, a therapist from a different treatment service, described what happened at the meeting as mutual 'undermining'. His observations of the interaction between the social worker and the psychologist were as follows:

> What struck me was that there was a lot of anger in the group of course, between [the psychologist] and [the social worker] almost to the point of undermining…that was the impression I got, that one was undermining the other… [the psychologist] was too preoccupied actually with his own therapeutic reputation shall we say… He didn't feel it was handled the way he wanted it, but if a group of people are working together for a particular goal, then they must work as a team… I thought he was a bit childish actually, in how he sort of handled it…

'Supporting one another in times of trouble' was identified by the interviewees as a key element of inter-professional co-operation. At the earlier mentioned case conference on the M family when it had been recently discovered that agreements between the family and the Health Board had been seriously breached, the attitude of the psychologist who had been treating one of the children was quite unhelpful, according to the acting social work manager:

> There was an overwhelming air of 'I told you so'... There was an air of 'You don't know what you're doing' which I found a bit unpleasant to say the least, and then [the psychologist's] prima donna stuff about...his therapy having been ruined and destroyed and that he wasn't even willing to engage in discussion about that... None of that struck me as being the sort of co-operation or the sort of co-operative stance that people at a case conference should be taking when dealing with extremely difficult and dangerous situations like this. It wasn't very helpful or supportive.

As the following section illustrates, 'fall-out' from these processes had a significant impact on the outcome of case conference decisions and plans.

Conference plans

Case conference discussions appeared to veer towards outlining plans, rather than making definite decisions about how child protection measures could be carried out. In certain cases, there were foregone con-clusions. Although there was usually some discussion as to the feasibility and adequacy of these prior arrangements, they were usually endorsed by the conference.

In general, conference plans included conditional commitments from participating professionals, for example, to secure short-term or part-time foster care arrangements, arrange therapy, or to have children assessed to determine the extent of sexual abuse they may have suffered. In two con-ferences, the initial approach to parents was planned and negotiated, and in others agreement was made to carry out definite tasks, like writing to the housing department, sending reports to other agencies, the continuance of regular home visiting, or the recruitment of a family support worker. However, the negotiation of plans was by no means an automatic or easily resolved process; on the contrary, it appeared to be difficult and complex, again dominated by exchanges about whose responsibility it was to carry out tasks, how long agencies were prepared to stay involved, difficulty about allocating staff and accessing resources, shortage of residential and foster placements, and likelihood of parental co-operation. Many of the plans made were quite tentative, and contingency arrangements were rarely addressed, apart from agreements about re-convening the conferences.

Undoubtedly, interactional processes and relationships had quite a significant impact on the way in which the recommendations were understood and appreciated, and how arrangements were agreed for their execution. When participants were interviewed after the child protection conferences, it was obvious that in many instances they were unclear about plans or had reservations about them, or experienced confusion as to what exactly was supposed to happen next.

For example, a conference concluded that further investigation should be carried out into previous complaints by neighbours that a mother had physically abused her children, and that respite foster care should be arranged for the children. However, the later interviews with participants revealed a level of confusion about who was to carry out the tasks; the chairperson thought it was the social worker who co-ordinated the family support service, the acting social work manager was unsure, and the social worker from the child psychiatric service realised that she didn't know either: 'I was clear that fostering was suggested but I wasn't clear when it would be possibly happening and who would inform me about it...' This was contrary to what her colleague thought: 'I think we sought clarity and got it, and defined, twice or three times what steps were being taken'.

One of the aims of another conference was to co-ordinate the police investigation of the abuse with other interventions that were to take place with the family, so that people were clear about their different roles. The chairperson believed that this had been achieved, though not without difficulty. But the Garda involved later revealed that she had no idea what other professionals were going to do in the case. When asked if she was clear what everybody agreed, she replied, 'Not particularly to be honest... I [only] knew what I was going to do'.

Other participants revealed in the interviews that they were not always satisfied with conference recommendations. A police officer who agreed to pursue a prosecution of a mother who continuously left her children on their own had reservations about what he considered was a misguided plan:

I mean... I have no problem with this prosecution, but my question is... I'd love to find out at the end of the day, what will it do for [the mother]? Will it make her amend her ways? I somehow don't think it will, because I feel unfortunately...this person...pals around with people who have come into contact with the Gardaí, so it's no big deal for them... It may be me that's naive, because I haven't an awful lot of experience of dealing with child abandonment, but... Well, you see we [the police] tend to think of these things as in the realm of the social workers... They deal with that, that's their problem, we notify them, and they take it from there.

Corby (1987), in a study carried out in England during the early 1980s, noted that the assumption that there was agreement over case conference norms meant that most conference decisions were made with apparent consensus. I would suggest that in the conferences observed in this study there was tacit agreement over avoidance of overt conflict, and the consensus which was reached was 'apparent' but very fragile indeed, as borne out by the failure of participants to follow up many of the undertakings made. There was, in some cases, an assumption that decisions carried some weight, as in the decision that a letter would go to the housing department from the conference, but it was clear that the power of the conference to compel practitioners particularly, but not exclusively, those outside the statutory system, to carry out certain acts, was very weak indeed.

Conclusion

The previous chapters have demonstrated the criteria that were employed to decide whether or not referrals to the social work team warranted investigation, and the sort of judgements that were reached on the basis of information gained as a result of investigation. It has been shown that certain measures were employed by social workers to discount the seriousness of reports. All these strategies were heavily influenced by a number of dynamics including: the necessity to keep the workload manageable, reluctance to invade family privacy, pessimism about the potential of 'chronic' families to change and a strong motive to share the responsibility for dealing with child abuse issues with other child care agencies and professionals. Judgements appeared to centre on the incidents and concerns that had, out of all the adversities experienced by families, crossed the threshold into 'child protection' business. However, it was clear that a number of adjudications were made on an impressionistic and moralistic basis, focusing very much on the attitude of mothers who, by their co-operation, their acknowledged culpability and contrition, and confirmation of their protective capacities, satisfied the investigating worker.

Observation of child protection conferences, which are deemed so central to 'good' child protection practice, provided a unique opportunity to observe these dynamics in action, in a more explicit fashion and in a wider context. It must again be stressed here that child protection conferences were generally regarded as useful by the participants in this research. However, they identified a number of weaknesses in the process, which were also visible to me as an observer; this chapter has concentrated mainly on conferences where those were most obvious.

Assessment norms similar to those followed by statutory social workers in the early stages of investigation were also visible at child protection conferences, but this time the moral reasoning focused more on the use of deservedness, co-operation, and reliability as tariffs for the allocation of resources. Farmer and Owen (1995) have noted the way in which anxiety at case conferences is managed by adherence to procedures, which often gives the false impression that major problems are being resolved. A similar type of adherence to the 'official' agenda was observable at the Ballyowen conferences.

The consequent narrowness of the discussions was, however, perceived by the participants to exclude potentially useful functions. These included conceptualisation about different aspects of abuse, which could be linked in a theoretical way to family dynamics, which in turn could promote insights into the causes of the child care concerns under discussion. As one worker put it, the 'business of almost following the format that's been laid down' made for a 'very hollow conference' that ignores 'the issues'. However, the parameters of the formula were defended by the person normally responsible for chairing the meetings, who felt that 'general discussions' were better 'left to another forum'. There is an interesting parallel here with a theme noted in the previous chapter, where the workers would now and again rebel against the discourse they felt compelled to operate in, and were kept 'in check' by a colleague or manager.

The deficiencies in the nature of the discussion, not surprisingly, appeared to affect the quality of the proposed plans, which in a small number of cases were deemed unclear and unrealistic. However, the most noticeable dynamic in the conferences was the tension between professionals, which undoubtedly impacted on the entire endeavour. As Reder *et al.* (1993, p.67) have argued, interactional processes are affected by issues such as 'attendances and absences, chairing, alliances, hierarchy and projection'. In the Ballyowen case conferences, hidden agendas were visible, the use of professional stereotyping and the influence of exaggerated hierarchies were equally obvious. Their presence, and their impact, was confirmed by the practitioners themselves.

In general, many of the negative interactions seemed to centre on the notion of responsibility for the investigation and management of child abuse, which was frequently batted about, and which the conferences did little to clarify. The failure to openly address some of these issues led to confusion as to who should execute the agreed plans. Given that the (unacknowledged) purpose of almost half of the case conferences was to address inter-agency and inter-professional differences, this is a paradoxical finding.

The case conference, according to Reder *et al.* (1993, p.68) 'is a brief episode in the continuous inter-relationships between members of the network'. Undoubtedly, inter-agency and inter-professional dynamics are fundamental to professional behaviour right through the career of a case. In order to elucidate these and other processes at work throughout the chronology of the cases under study, the next chapter will look at the longer term aspects of child protection work.

Chapter Five

The Evolution of Case 'Careers'
Medium to Long-Term Child Protection Work

This chapter considers the patterns or themes in child protection practice that become more visible as the careers of the cases involved in this study develop. In doing so, it focuses on the child abuse referrals that, after investigation, were deemed to require further social work intervention. As Yin (1994) points out, one of the advantages of the case study design is its capacity to convince the reader that evidence has been collected exhaustively by the length of time spent in the field. Equally, the analysis of cases over an extended period provides the opportunity to use iterative explanation building to facilitate the emergence of new knowledge.

We look first at the characteristics of these cases and then go on to examine the elements of medium to long-term child protection work, using one case in particular to demonstrate the processes involved. This phase of the research process concentrates on material gleaned from the various accounts given by the practitioners in interviews, consolidated by the data that emerged during the review conferences, and the interviews that were later held with some of the parents. As case careers developed, the social workers assigned to them were interviewed at intervals of approximately six weeks to two months following allocation and immediately following review case conferences. In addition, a final interview was carried out with practitioners in relation to each of the cases still open at the end of the 12-month fieldwork period. Fourteen of the child abuse allegations reported to Ballyowen during the first phase of the fieldwork period were allocated to social workers on the Health Board community care team. Three others were managed by agencies outside the statutory service: two by multi-disciplinary treatment agencies, and one by a voluntary agency for children with disabilities. The specific 'risks' or concerns involved in the allocated cases are detailed in Figure 5.1; many of them were common to more than one case.

- 'Unfinished business' regarding child sexual abuse, including validation and/or treatment
- Evidence and admission by mother of physical abuse to child
- Depressed condition of child
- Sexual vulnerability of child
- Mother's excessive drinking as a cause of neglect and danger
- History of separation combined with current concern about neglect
- Placement breakdown associated with evidence and admission of physical abuse
- Evidence of children being left unsupervised (by their mother) on a continuous basis
- Age-inappropriate expectations of children by mother
- Behaviour management problems leading to excessive and inappropriate discipline
- Mother's continuing relationship with a violent partner

Figure 5.1 Specific child protection concerns in the allocated cases

The 'child abuse' lens

Whether or not the workers had volunteered to take on cases or the social work manager had acted prescriptively to allocate them, the initial approach to work in the different situations was taken within a common framework and appeared to be underpinned by a 'reactive' rather than a 'proactive' principle. Chapter Three has already illustrated that with one exception, the only new referrals to the social work department in the fieldwork period which were allocated for ongoing work, apart from those which were given to a student, were child protection cases, or at least appeared to contain child abuse concerns. Even when other family crises were present, unless they conformed to the 'norm' of child abuse, they were not normally offered an ongoing service. While family support services have been developed, albeit in a fragmented fashion in Ireland over the past five years (McKeown 2000) there remains evidence that the narrow child abuse norm still operated to filter cases for several years after the fieldwork for this study was conducted (Buckley 2002). Similar trends have been observed in the UK where Tunstill and Aldgate (2000) have argued that the nature of statutory responsibility is frequently misunderstood by social services departments and is still seen as synonymous with child protection investigation.

The type of guidance generally offered in child protection procedures tends to portray the process of investigation and assessment of child abuse as a series of sequential steps, each one either discounting or accumulating concern about a situation which leads the investigating workers to the next logical action. The validity of each stage is assumed. However, closer study of this process reveals that the reality of child protection practice is quite different. Previous chapters have illustrated the various influences on the investigative process that combine to construct the type of child abuse case that is likely to elicit a response. These include the interpretations of events that are offered by the various agents involved, all of whom have their own agendas in relation to the disposal of the child abuse concern. Not least of these were their differential notions of what constituted 'child abuse' and the agents' own aspirations to either avoid or control involvement in the process. It is not surprising therefore, that when the actual facts of a case became more visible, the new 'construction' differed considerably from the way it first appeared.

Some of the cases that were allocated for further work had been subjected to very little prior or first-hand investigation, but in most instances, accounts had been offered that made them appear to contain fairly serious risks for children. As the perception of these risks either diminished or increased, the original plans for intervention inevitably changed and sometimes the concerns were re-framed. For example, three of the allocated cases involved allegations about child sexual abuse that had been endorsed by the investigation, but were later discounted. Another involved suspicions of physical and emotional abuse which, when put in a fuller context, appeared less sinister. Likewise, in a case where the mother had been seen behaving drunkenly on the corridor outside her flat with a child on her own inside, the assigned worker actually found that the referral 'scenario' had been reported without some significant contextual information and, in reality, had not been as dramatic. He also found that the ongoing 'risk' to the children was greatly diminished by the strong and supportive family network involved, though they were undoubtedly suffering adversities that affected their welfare and quality of life.

A sizeable number of the children involved in the different cases had not, in fact, suffered identifiable harm or injury. This finding is consistent with the data collected by Parton *et al.* (1997) and later in an Irish study by Ferguson and O'Reilly (2001) and belies the notion that families in the child protection system are in any way exceptional, or that the hazards to which the children are exposed are not common to many children in the population. The act of re-framing these cases occasionally de-stabilised the basis on which they had been allocated. For example, in the 'neglect' case quoted above, the social worker had started to address the family's various difficulties with them, and planned to continue to do so. He was apprehensive, however, that the diminution of 'abuse' meant his work might not be 'legitimate':

> I find it actually a very interesting case to work on, but what would concern me, with the pressure of work... I could actually be called off the case now that it's being managed and I don't think that would be a good idea.

Another case was initially referred because of the public health nurse's concerns about physical and emotional abuse of the children. Quite soon after the case was allocated, the Health Board social worker who had taken it on commented that while the mother was experiencing difficulty with one child's behaviour and there were relationship problems between herself and her partner, there were no child protection issues. Again, the question of the legitimacy of keeping this case open cropped up:

...if I was bringing it up to supervision, and there is a waiting list, you know, I would be told more or less to refer it to [a treatment service] for family therapy.

The above examples illustrate the limited focus initially applied to longer term interventions and the almost secretive way in which preventative and proactive work would be carried out when the 'child abuse' issues diminished. However, as one interviewee in the study suggested, this trend may have been perpetuated not by management, but by the practitioners themselves who had internalised the 'child abuse' bias:

If people don't come in with their eye in a sling, the social workers have no interest in it... We're whipped up into the notion that 'that's not our problem...' We're very narrow in our own role.

But whatever the agency claimed as its 'official' approach to child protection work, once a case had passed the hurdle of allocation, the social workers tended to respond according to their own notion of appropriate intervention. While they were often dependent on other professionals and agencies to provide different services, they were largely responsible for the day-to-day management of their own practice, with social work being largely, as Pithouse (1987) termed it, an 'invisible trade'.

The other theme that becomes more visible during the case 'careers' is the link between a co-operative attitude from the parents, normally the mothers, and the maintenance of social work involvement. In one case, a mother and one-year-old child had been referred for a second time when police had reportedly found her and her known-to-be-violent ex-partner fighting on the street. Both were allegedly intoxicated, with the child nearby in his buggy. The incident had initially sounded very dramatic, but its urgent status had been exaggerated, in the view of the social worker who finally got it:

This situation is really not that terribly serious, do you know what I mean, somehow or other it's been built up... When you actually look at the incidents that occurred, they're very minor... You see, I have a feeling that somehow the services are very involved with this woman because she co-operates... If she was less co-operative and more hostile, it could go the other way, the child might have ended up in care, but apart from the incidents, if she was a bit more hostile and a bit more assertive, and aggressive, against the services, I think she could probably have kept them further away and we'd know less about it...

He was clearly describing a case where the 'operational perspectives' (Cleaver and Freeman 1995) of the mother and the child protection system were close enough to reach a mutual understanding. This study demonstrates evidence of the pivotal position of such agreement in determining the feasibility of longer term work.

Ongoing work: child protection plans

Five of the fourteen cases allocated to the social work team had been the subject of child protection conferences. Programmes or plans had been set out at these, though as Chapter Four has illustrated, the short-term and unrealistic nature of some of the plans (often undermined by the serious inter-agency tensions that prevailed at the time) meant that they did not uniformly provide a framework for action. The child protection guidelines in operation at the time of the fieldwork for this study gave very limited advice on assessment, child protection plans or longer term work, nor did they compel the review of work with children considered to be at risk. Most of the time, the social workers had to devise their own strategies, with or without input from either managers or colleagues. However, the interviews that I carried out with the practitioners revealed that they had all mapped out some idea of how to proceed with their work, and the goals they were hoping to achieve with their clients. The plans were generally comprised of the following elements, some of which were common to more than one case:

- further assessment, to be followed by therapy
- 'work' with mothers and children concerning discipline and other parenting skills
- 'work' on family relationships
- arranging out of home care where decisions had been made to separate children and families

- ongoing support of out of home placements together with facilitating parental access
- co-ordination of treatment services
- provision of practical support
- individual counselling and parenting work
- direct work with children
- advocacy with a range of welfare and other organisations

Some examples include behavioural work with a mother and her children, as described by the worker:

> ...basically it's temper tantrums and the mother just not being able to deal with them, and when she does, dealing with them inappropriately, in a violent sort of way, hitting out and then the child actually screaming, creating concerns for neighbours, and the screams, from [the mother's] account don't reconcile with the amount of hitting if you know what I mean... I think the mother is aware that the way she is managing the behaviour is not appropriate and is alerting services including public health nurses and ourselves, but she said she is frustrated, she is doing her best and I think there are ways in which we could work together with regard to managing that behaviour.

Another example concerned a lone mother who had alcohol related problems:

> It appeared fairly clear to me that [the mother] needed social work inter-vention in a supportive way, around issues relating to parenting, general concerns around welfare and housing...drinking was also a very perti-nent one as well.

According to the data available, the actual 'interventions' consisted in some instances of administrative work, such as writing letters, making appoint-ments on behalf of families for assessment and treatment services, setting up placements and negotiating with management over financial arrangements to support them and making arrangements with schools. Discussions took place, mostly on the telephone, with other practitioners who were involved with the families, such as public health nurses, doctors, teachers and so on. In addition, consultations took place on an informal basis between the social workers themselves, and on both formal and informal bases between the social workers and the social work manager and senior area medical officer.

Only a certain amount of work was done, therefore, in direct contact with service users. Some of the personal contact with the families took place in the office, though the majority of it happened in their own homes. Little account was demonstrated by the practitioners, either of the known effectiveness of interventions or of method or outcome goals, that are seen to be so fundamental to interventions (McDonald 2001). While some of the work could undoubtedly be labelled 'therapeutic', it was not possible to classify it in terms of models or frameworks for practice, as the remainder of this chapter will demonstrate. This type of practice was not unique; in later studies carried out in different Health Board regions, evidence of child protection plans in social workers' case files was very scarce (Buckley *et al.* 1997; Horwath 2001).

'Monitoring'

Given that all the cases were allocated on the basis of some concerns, however vague, about the safety and protection of children, the 'monitoring' of risk could be expected to comprise an important element in the social work activity. Parton *et al.* (1997) found in their study that most of the longer term work with clients tended to be around 'risk management'. In this book, the 'child abuse' elements in the various cases in this study were often later mitigated or appeared unsubstantiated once the social worker had become involved, and the work frequently took a different course. Yet it was still time-limited (as will be shown later) and framed according to the presence or absence of risks.

In several cases, the social workers followed a trend, noted in earlier chapters, of delegating the 'monitoring' of risk to other professionals. For example, a 16-year-old boy went to stay in a hostel that the social worker felt rendered him less vulnerable to risky behaviour than when he was living at home and the care staff there kept the social worker in touch with his well-being. Another of the social workers used schools to gauge how particular children were getting on. He believed this to be a less intrusive way of keeping in touch with the situation, but also a more effective one:

...children spend more time in school being supervised than they do by social workers or by parents. They are in school from nine to three, there is no way in which we as professionals can observe children for that length of time or in fact do parents, so they give you a good insight into what is going on for the child at an emotional, psychological, sexual and intellectual level. All of these are areas which we are concerned about.

This chapter, however, in keeping with the aim of the study to explore and expose the less discernible aspects of child protection work, is not so much concerned with actually describing the *nature* of the work undertaken, than it is with explaining the frameworks through which the various interventions were carried out, and the influences which combined to determine outcomes. The narrowness of the 'child abuse' paradigm has already been described. Other significant issues that became visible were the way in which knowledge was utilised by the practitioners, the focus on mothers, and the persistence of inter-agency and inter-professional tensions.

Social workers' use of theory

There was at the time this study was undertaken, already a body of literature on both the aetiology and effects of child abuse, which utilises sociological theory, family systems theory, attachment and other psychological explanations to illustrate the process through which neglect and other abuses take place (e.g., Parton 1985; Reder *et al.* 1993; Crittenden 1993; Corby 1993). Additionally, the long-term effects of abuse on children, particularly in relation to academic, developmental, social and behavioural deficits had been researched (e.g. Finkelhor 1984; Glaser and Frosh 1988; Claussen and Crittenden 1991). Research had been conducted, particularly in relation to neglect, showing that many of the negative consequences of these forms of maltreatment are more psychologically disabling than those of physical abuse or sexual abuse (Crouch and Milner 1993). Yet despite what was known and understood about child abuse, there was little if any evidence in this study of social workers acknowledging the dimensions of the problem, or making any serious attempt to get to grips with it.

A similar trend is apparent in the literature. Thorpe (1994, p.196) for example, considering the 'overrepresentation of poor and disadvantaged people' in child abuse statistics, argues that 'child protection' does little to improve the lot of many children who come into its net, and in fact performs poorly in relation to 'neglect' cases. The reason, he explains, is because the 'technology' and 'knowledge base' that is constructed around child abuse does not represent the majority of those who actually come into contact with the system. Stevenson (1996, p.13) explains the 'neglect of neglect' in the same terms, but also highlights the links between neglect and poverty, and the way that social workers have become used to certain families 'bumping along the bottom'. Perceiving the parents to be under intolerable strain practitioners, according to Stevenson, 'are reluctant to make the judgements which lead to the finding of neglect' (p.16). The social workers in Ballyowen were clearly operating within the same parameters, which they used as channels through which to divert families from the system.

However, the assumption that practising social workers do not 'use' theory was challenged by Paley (1987), who has argued that accounting for practice in theoretical terms tends to be situation specific. Using the language of the sociology of science, Paley describes the type of discourse in which social workers explain their actions as a 'contingent repertoire' rather than an 'empiricist' style which would theoretically 'account' for their practices. In this study, although the practitioners did not all identify their activities within 'professional' theoretical frameworks or models of intervention, their contingent or natural accounts of practice did appear to portray the goals they were actually trying to achieve with their clients, and linked these to the causes of the alleged abuse.

Direct interventions with clients were outlined in terms of named, and more often unnamed, pieces of 'work'. The newly qualified social worker described some of his methods as 'behaviour modification', and identified his approach in a particular case as 'systemic'. Both he and another worker said that they used 'brief therapy'[1] principles with certain clients. The more experienced worker was less sure of its effectiveness and applicability in her situation:

Well, I was trying to do... I had it earmarked as a case for brief therapy...and I did try to use those principles at the start by sort of trying to turn it around and help her to establish what positives she had done... I didn't feel it was universally successful.

Another worker described how a combination of her reflections on the specific aspects of the situation, and her knowledge of theory, influenced her decisions about how to manage the case:

The other thing that I have done, I think since thinking about the family a little bit more and reading a little bit more around sexual abuse and also the contact from the school and some of the things the guidance teacher was saying... That made me think a little bit more about the whole context of safety and protection for the children.

The social worker with a 'neglectful' lone mother described her work:

Well, I have sort of attempted to encourage her to talk about the past, the way she feels about herself living there... I have attempted to give her time to talk. Her older son was killed and his anniversary came up and I tried to get her to talk about that...

The social worker for the mother with the violent partner and a problem with alcohol had identified the root of the client's problems:

I feel I'm dealing with some fairly deep rooted personality factors in [the mother]... There are things that are drawing her towards destructive relationships and self destructive behaviours and things which I'm not sure she fully understands herself and I'm not sure...how shiftable they might be... There's two issues, the drink and the relationship and that's a dynamic and the problem is for her to somehow gain some understanding of that which will somehow help her to convince people that she can now control it better. And that's what we're after...

One of the other social workers described how her methods of work evolved:

I know that just because of what you've picked up along the way and what you have learned, at different stages, you bring with you to each stage, but I haven't sat down and said I'm using a...family therapy model... I mean...in the family, I have been very much responding on an individual level to what I felt each person or situation needed and I know there's stuff behind that but I'm not specifically looking back and saying

'Oh, that's such a model and this is something else…' I would think that over the years obviously I have learned a lot and I think from when I was in college there would have been models and all that kind of baloney…and I think I work in a particular way because I have been in this job for so long and I have absorbed a lot… I'm sure it's based on theory, maybe at some points along the way…but I don't avidly read books on theory when I go home…

There were also examples of what Stevenson (1997) describes as 'anti-intellectualism', which she explains as a reluctance to make explicit the place which knowledge or theory should have in professional activity. For example, one social worker, when asked if he was using a particular type or method of intervention or model of work responded, 'No, I deliberately don't!'

A number of explanations have been offered for the absence of theory, or critical reflection, in child protection work. Stevenson (1989) has argued that social workers, bruised by critiques of their use of psychodynamic theory, have been nervous of using it. She links her observations to the powerful impact of sociological theories, particularly those linked with material deprivation and disadvantage. She suggests locating the cause of child abuse in a parent/child relationship ignores the wider social and structural dimensions of the problem, (e.g. poverty and disadvantage) and is antithetical to the way in which social workers like to perceive themselves and be perceived. However, as she points out, this can mean that social workers are left without 'theoretical subplots' (p.162) that can reside within more generalised social theories of social functioning.

Focus on mothers and avoidance of fathers

Parton *et al.*'s (1997) theory about the construction of child protection in terms of maternal responsibility and mothers' capacity to protect has already been demonstrated in this study. When longer term work is examined, mothers appear to remain the principal focus of workers. Where risks were still apparent, the 'monitoring' was frequently left to mothers. In one case where the mother was actually considered the neglectful parent, the context was slightly different, but the process was similar. The mother's drinking was the identified cause of the children's maltreatment.

Due to her previous 'parental incorrigibility' (Dingwall *et al.* 1983), the interventions made were of quite a legalistic nature, in terms of having her barred from the family home. The social worker was aware that the father was drinking as well, but unlike his wife, he was not regarded as culpable for the neglect of his children.

This is an interesting example of Milner's (1996) concept of 'mitigation' whereby men are not necessarily expected to be in charge of their own emotional responses, or have responsibility for nurturance, care and emotional management of families. While the father remained ostensibly the main 'carer', interviews with the social worker in the case revealed that she had less contact with him than she had with the woman living next door to the family, who acted in a mediating role, keeping the social worker informed, and providing support to the children. This woman provided the children with 'space away from home...huge support' and acted, as the social worker described her 'like another agency'.

In nine of the fourteen cases allocated to Health Board social workers, the mother's cohabitee was either living in the family home, or was strongly connected with the family, with frequent access to the children. Even so, there were only four cases in which adult male clients were actively engaged with social workers. One of these was closed early on in the fieldwork period – there was only one contact with the family, which consisted of a joint interview. In two other cases, estranged fathers were brought into some of the sessions.

Milner (1993) has cited evidence to illustrate the strategies used by social workers to deal with violent fathers which legitimate their concentration on mothers. In this study, it was noticeable that where fathers/mother's partners did not voluntarily present themselves, they were not actively pursued by the social workers. In the aforementioned case where a mother kept returning to her violent partner and her child was, at one point, slightly injured during an assault, the father was naturally implicated in ongoing concern about the child. One of the ongoing risks in this case was created by the mother's pattern of returning to this violent man again and again. Yet no efforts were made by the social worker to contact him at any point, and the responsibility was allocated to the mother to 'work on the relationship'.

In a different case, the central problem, according to the duty social worker that first took the referral, was the mother's 'stress':

> All the men in her life have been alcoholic, which is significant... She has also been physically abused by the two lovers in her life, her husband and this guy...[who] is drinking as well.

The social worker's main concern was that the mother was 'taking her upset out on the children... She's a woman who has a very short fuse'. Other referral information provided by the public health nurse suggested that 'she gets less able to cope with her own irritability and anger and frustration when stress gets tough for her'. When this case was allocated, the social worker used star charts to help the mother manage her daughter's behaviour, but never at any stage met the violent partner who lived in the family home because 'he was never present when I was there...he was always out'.

The entry of a 16-year-old boy into voluntary care was precipitated by an assault by his mother and her male cohabitee. The man was never involved in any ongoing work, according to the social worker 'because he was moving out of the family home' although he was still there at the end of the fieldwork period.

The focus on mothers also illustrated a paradoxical element in the way that female parents are generally not only regarded as the 'responsible' parents, but inevitably the 'appropriate' persons to care for children. Featherstone (1996) alludes to the contradiction inherent in a universalist feminist approach which seeks to portray women as 'victims' rather than 'villains', and to use gender analyses in a reductionist rather than an explanatory fashion when it comes to addressing mothers' maltreatment of their children. Wise (1995) makes a similar point, arguing that a feminist approach becomes problematic when viewed in the context of child protection work in a statutory setting, where the children are more vulnerable than their mothers. This type of conflict was evident in a case where the mother had twice falsely (by her own admission) accused her estranged husband of sexually abusing their children. The social worker, who was male, displayed some frustration with the way the mother's and father's roles were constructed and interpreted by the principal agencies involved, including the women's refuge:

> There are a lot of gender issues here… We are all emphasising, and the court is very receptive to the idea that this woman is physically and mentally abused, but nobody has actually taken on board the manipulative and violent means by which this woman has achieved her ends… The dad in this case is being a victim of feminism and I think social workers have fallen into this trap of the 'poor woman'.

In the view of the social worker, the mother was aggravating the father's attempts to maintain satisfactory relationships with the children, and was using them as a weapon to vent her anger against him. Interviewed again three months later, the worker still felt strongly about the way his attempts to involve the father 'in some meaningful way' were:

> …obstructed by an extremely manipulative woman…knowing at the end of the day that she could cry wolf and the whole system would align itself with her… I'm talking about the legal system and say, agencies like the refuge… They wouldn't take into account the role of the father.

As Featherstone (1997, p.424) argues, there is currently a growing recognition that 'women's and men's subjectivities are not stable, essential or fixed', and the notion of a woman as 'primarily, or purely, victim or nurturant' is not acceptable any longer. The ready acceptance by what the social worker called 'the whole system' that the mother was a perpetual 'victim' acted, it appears, to obscure her emotional manipulation of her children.

The tendency for child protection workers to focus on mothers has been acknowledged in the literature and professionals have been urged to raise their awareness of the importance of working with fathers, not only because of their possible culpability for child abuse, but because failure to engage them could be to ignore a potential resource and strength to provide support to vulnerable children (Ryan 2000; Daniel and Taylor 2001). In the meantime, research continues to demonstrate the gendered nature of the work (Ferguson and O' Reilly 2001; Horwath 2001).

Inter-agency co-operation re-visited

Many of the inter-professional conflicts impacting on the early stages of investigation and assessment have been illustrated in chapters Two and Four, but when the later stages in the careers of the cases in this study are examined, it can be seen that the level of co-ordinated work carried out between the different professionals in the network diminished considerably as time went by. This tendency has been identified by Hallett (1995) who found that most information exchange took place in the early phases of referral and investigation but declined in the later stages.

When particular cases are examined, the way in which the notion of interdisciplinary work becomes more like 'romantic fiction' (Wise 1989) becomes visible. Examples abound of breakdowns in communication. For example, the women's refuge neglected to inform the social worker that a mother who had agreed to stay there for the protection of her child had broken her contract by leaving. Little contact had been maintained between the Health Board social worker and the alcohol treatment service that the same mother was attending, so that her non-attendance there was not known. Agreements about joint plans, some of which had been made at child protection conferences, were frequently disrupted. For example, the police officer who agreed to prosecute a neglectful mother still had not contacted her two months later. Despite a commitment from staff in a special school attended by a 13-year-old boy to carry out joint work with the Health Board social worker, the child was quite abruptly expelled after a misdemeanour. The statutory social workers were very critical of the other agencies involved, attributing for example, the above mentioned boy's expulsion to inflexibility on the part of the school and the fact that 'he didn't fit in with their model', and accusing the women's refuge and the alcohol treatment unit of disowning responsibility: 'They didn't see themselves as having any role in the child protection issue'.

The case involving CM, a 16-year-old girl who had been sexually abused by her father has already been used to illustrate a 'text book' scenario in terms of the way the case was initially approached and the type of response it received. It now provides a good example of how early aspirations towards inter-agency co-ordination can become extremely 'thin' as a case unfolds, but it also represents a number of the other complex elements of child protection work, encapsulating many of those that were also visible in the other cases.

Case example: the M case

Mrs M fitted into the notion of the 'non-abusing mother' that has received much attention in feminist writing on child protection (Parton 1990; Hooper 1992; Wise 1989, 1995). Hooper's study demonstrated the slow, painful journey experienced by mothers coming to terms with the abuse of their children, whereby they move through the phases of 'not knowing', 'suspecting' and 'knowing'. Explained in terms of bereavement and loss, the process, particularly the final stage, can take months for full resolution. The irony, as Hooper explained it, is that during this period mothers are faced with the onerous responsibility for protecting and healing their children whilst still subject to grief for their children's trust and innocence, their self-esteem as caring parents and their former relationships. This burden is often linked with economic insecurity. During this time, they are often subjected to opprobrium from their extended families and community, and subject to emotional pressure from the abuser. Yet in this context they are expected, according to the criteria normally used for assessment, to act 'appropriately' in relation to the child protection system (Parton *et al.* 1997). Mrs M's own perspective will be more fully examined in the following chapter. However, suffice it to say at this point that her experience could be described quite accurately within Hooper's framework.

As Hooper suggests, the ability of non-abusing mothers to come to terms with their losses, and gather the resources they need to heal themselves and their children, is significantly affected by the quality of support offered to them. Yet the relationship between themselves and child protection workers is subject to several complicating effects, including the aforementioned unrealistic expectations of professionals, but also the 'social control' function of workers. One of the solutions that Hooper suggests, which is also endorsed by Farmer and Owen (1995) and Gibbons *et al.* (1995), is the allocation of a different worker once the investigation phase is complete. The M's social worker had requested a co-worker at the outset, but nobody had been free to take on the work. The social worker was left, therefore, to combine an authoritative statutory role, which she exercised by getting the father to move out by using the threat of removing the children if he didn't comply, with a helping supportive role, attempting to enable the family to come to terms with what had happened.

This dual identity is generally difficult for social workers and parents (Corby 1987; Farmer and Owen 1995; Gibbons *et al.* 1995), but as Hooper's study shows, it is particularly so in such a sensitive context. The social worker for the M case was aware of the non-abusing mother's need for support, yet worried about the ultimate safety of the children:

> A lot of work has been with mother, supporting her to support the rest…and I wonder, you know, am I not being sensitive enough to the family's need for the father's presence…and then I put on the child protection hat, and I'm trying to balance, that's the difficult thing about all this, trying to balance, trying to take this as a very individual, very unique family and listening to what they have to say about their own experience…and trying to fit that with our very global policies and our very global knowledge around sexual abuse, and sometimes I think I'm being too hard, and sometimes I think I'm being absolutely led and sucked into this family… It's a dilemma.

The social worker had, in her view, managed the early stages of the investigation and assessment without much difficulty, but four months into the case, she was suffering from some self-doubt about the efficacy of her interventions. She had found the early phase of the casework 'busy' in terms of arranging assessments, meetings, referring family members for therapy, but now that the active phase was over, she began to question her input to the case:

> Have I done this in the most effective way possible, should I have been digging rather than supporting, do I have enough material myself to make any kind of an assessment around risk to these children?…

She was concerned about the 'silence' between the mother and the children at home, who were not talking to each other about what had happened. In order to achieve what she described as a 're-alignment' of the situation, she decided to involve the father in some joint sessions with the rest of the family. The social worker was very positive about the possibilities these meetings opened up. However, at a review conference, a conflict arose between herself and the treatment agency working with the father, based on the agency's objection to the inclusion of the father in sessions with his children. This did not fit in with the model of therapy favoured by them and they threatened to exclude the father from their treatment programme if these sessions continued.

This process reflected a phenomenon which Reder *et al.* (1993, p.73) have termed 'polarisation', whereby fixed beliefs dominate the practice of one agency, creating mistrust of others and inhibiting collaborative work. According to the belief adopted by the treatment agency, incestuous fathers must be prevented from having any further contact with the children they have abused. In effect, they considered that the social worker was colluding with the abuse by including the father in meetings with the children and implicitly allowing him to continue his manipulation of them. The social worker who had felt very positive about the family sessions, was left quite confused and a bit sceptical about this stipulation, considering that the treatment agency had an over-inflated view of their capacity to deal with the father:

> I don't know if there is any reconciliation on the two approaches, it did cause me a fair bit of grief... I went home and I really soul searched, and I thought, God, you know...could we really have gone ahead with those family meetings without the father?... Would the family have had a better opportunity to talk and to elaborate some kind of story if he weren't there?...and you know, I don't know the answer to that... but... I have worked in a programme for sexual offenders in the States...

What the social worker described as the 'controversy' which arose at the review conference was all the more acute because a number of the other practitioners involved in the case had failed to attend, illustrating the way that co-ordinated work diminishes after a time:

> I was very disappointed because I have been planning this conference since the beginning of September...and the first time that everybody could come together was the 21st November, it was horrendous, and in the meantime you had this family waiting... We finally got a date that everybody could come on... I was hugely taken aback the day before the case conference we had a message from [the psychologist], who was very significant, that she couldn't attend...it meant that she wasn't partaking in any of the discussion around risk...around support... Her opinion

would have been very welcome on the controversy around including father…and for some reason or other the police didn't turn up, and there were no apologies, I don't know what that was about… I had asked [the counsellor] from the school to come but she didn't…

Following that conference, the social worker, having consulted with her line managers, reluctantly terminated the family meetings in order to facilitate the father's treatment. But again, after another three months, she felt extremely 'stuck'. This was not helped by her sense that she was getting no support from the other practitioners involved in the case and that a huge amount of the responsibility for the case fell on what she described as her 'personal shoulders':

> I really felt that after the last conference… I just felt that a huge amount of responsibility for this case, despite the other agencies who were involved, actually fell on my personal shoulders… While I know that the Health Board has responsibility for child abuse and co-ordination and all that, it was kind of like the other agencies involved were doing their little bits out here and weren't feeding into the centre… I would literally have to go chasing, spending weeks, to get them, just to say how are things going there, what do I need to know about progress or lack of it that will help me in the work with the family… It was kind of like, despite what we know about family dynamics and family systems in child sexual abuse, especially when it has been so pervasive, what I was finding now was that you had one person doing a little bit out here, quite…quite divorced from what was happening in the family, and you had another person doing a very significant amount out on the left field with no… I mean nobody ever phoned me up to say I'd like to give you an update, which had huge ramifications for the centre bit that I was trying to weave …and I wasn't a bit happy about that… I wasn't happy with how unavailable people were making themselves to sit down, even informally, to look at where do we go with the rest of the family… I just felt terribly alone and burdened by it…

Once again she had tried to arrange a review meeting but the unavailability of the required participants meant postponing it for over three months. She was also feeling very unconfident about her effectiveness though she felt that the lack of movement in the case was not entirely her fault:

Look, you know, it's not only my responsibility, it's others' responsibility as well...there's only so much you can do... Maybe it's time to regroup and get a few more other people involved.

As it happened, events overtook her uncertainty within a very short time and a 'crisis' broke in the case, when it was discovered that the father had been staying regularly in the family home again. At this point, the children were made the subject of court orders and placed in foster care.

Consideration of the M case at this point suggests a history (albeit brief) of fragmented practice where trust was breached on all sides, and which culminated in a tragic scenario of children being ultimately separated from their non-abusing mother. An official, inquiry-type examination of the practice in this case may have been very critical of the professionals involved. Yet as Wise (1989) demonstrated in an ethnographic study of child protection work and child abuse inquiries, it cannot be assumed that the career of a case follows any kind of normative framework. She identified four taken-for-granted theories about child abuse investigation:

- That child abuse has an identifiable set of causal predeterminants, such that it can be predicted.
- That child abuse is self evident, easily identifiable and anyone can tell when it is happening.
- That it is obvious what needs to be done in such cases and only incompetence prevents that from happening.
- That a key part of working competently involves effective interdisciplinary working and it is when this breaks down that problems occur. (p.467)

Analysis of the M case in this research concerns itself mainly with the latter two assumptions, though the first two also have some relevance. Wise (1989, p.465) was critical of child protection theories that ignore the 'complex and problematic social processes that exist in the relationship between social workers and clients'. The assumption that 'clear solutions' exist ignores, in her view, two important factors. One, that there is often simply no solution to a problem, and second, the weakness of assuming that clients will passively accept whatever suggestions are offered by the social worker.

Viewed within this framework, it is hardly surprising that the M's social worker was experiencing self-doubt after the first few 'busy' months where she was supplying essentially what Reder *et al.* (1993) would term 'concrete' solutions. In her anxiety to 'break the silence' in the family she may have chosen a model of work, family therapy, that could have further disempowered the mother and children and served indirectly to mitigate the abuser by its tendency to diffuse culpability and promote the notion of collusion (Hooper 1992). On the other hand, frameworks do exist through which, when well supported by supervision and skilled training, such a systems approach can usefully and successfully be applied in cases of intra-familial sexual abuse (Farrelly, Butler and O'Dalaigh 1993).

Another element of the 'clear solution' assumption identified by Wise suggests that parents will be malleable in relation to child protection interventions. Hooper (1992, pp.147–148) observes that mothers' experience of agency intervention depends on how far it accommodates and fits in with their own process of discovery and response. She describes how women's responses to the 'dual roles' of social workers, both monitoring and supporting, varied. In certain circumstances, Hooper argues, an agency's use of authority may reinforce the women's sense of entrapment and become the focus of a 'resistance strategy'. In the meantime, mothers can adopt what Reder *et al.* (1993) have termed 'disguised compliance', apparent co-operation which defuses the 'controlling' stance adopted by professional workers, and neutralises their authority. This complex response appears to have been adopted by Mrs M who allegedly gave the social worker no reason to think that she was breaching the agreement they had made in relation to her husband's access to the children. However, as time went by, the social worker had become aware of tensions growing between herself and the mother:

> I haven't been successful in moving the mother one iota, and at this stage she is quite antagonistic towards me…like we are the people who are keeping her husband out… I feel that they see me as the person who says a lot of no's…the big boss in some respects and the person with the stick. And that's difficult in terms of the work I'm trying to do with mother…

It is a difficult relationship where at one level you're trying to encourage her to look deeper at some of the issues for herself as a wife and a mother and a person in her own right and yet at the same time you know that you're also the person who makes the decisions... So it is quite a difficult relationship at that level.

Reder *et al.* (1993, p.99) observe the way in which parents, feeling that they are in precarious control of their lives, 'tighten the boundary' around themselves so that they effectively close off professionals. This may have happened between the social worker and Mrs M, as interview data indicated that the gaps between their meetings grew longer. Research also indicates a tendency for social workers to withdraw once the investigative stage is over. Hooper (1992) and Farmer and Owen (1995) found patterns whereby the involvement of agencies in the initial stages of child sexual abuse cases was not necessarily followed through with support in the aftermath despite the traumatic after effects of disclosure. The reasons, according to Farmer and Owen (1995), may be pressure on social workers' time, encouragement to close cases or because many social workers simply did not know how to advise parents. Nine months after the case was opened, the worker admitted that she hadn't seen Mrs M for over a month:

I have met her much less since the case conference for a number of reasons... I was beginning to find... I used to be able to see her about once every two weeks and I was finding that essentially I was repeating and repeating, and I couldn't get beyond the father coming home...no matter what I did...

The social worker's lack of alertness to the possibility that the father may have been gradually moving back into the family, together with the tapering off of her contact with them could also indicate another complex social process inherent in child protection work. This the erroneous tendency, described by Munro (1996, p.801), for social workers to hold on to a particular 'existing view' of the family, and only check information to see if it supported the preferred version of events.

Regardless of the precipitating reasons for the negative outcome in the case, the processes just described, together with those identified at various different stages in the case career, go some way to explain how a 'clear solution' would have been difficult to apply in this context. However, another significant factor that emerges from examination of the professional practice in this particular case relates to Wise's last assumption, the notion that inter-agency work is a 'key' part of working competently. As both this and the previous chapter have shown, a number of inter-agency and inter-professional issues impacted strongly on the management of this case. The assessment process, according to Reder *et al.* (1993, p.84), 'only has meaning when all information is pooled together and allowed to contribute to an overall and multi-dimensional picture'. The flow of information in this case was seriously impeded because of the interaction of a number of processes similar to those outlined in Reder *et al.*'s theoretical framework: some of the professionals from the various agencies were possibly over-burdened and did not have time to return phone calls, or attend meetings; the treatment agency was very tied into its own 'closed professional system' which did not allow permeability of its boundaries; the social worker was possibly equally bound into her own 'pervasive belief system' about the mother's capacity for compliance with agency injunctions; 'dormant rivalries' and 'exaggerated hierarchies' surfaced at various points, and all of these tensions combined, it appears, to exclude the subjects of concern, the mother and children.

In summary, the M case needs to be viewed in terms of the complex social and organisational processes that operate to a greater or lesser degree in all child protection work; despite the facility and efficiency with which initial interventions were put into practice, this case was no more immune than any other to the potential distortions which can occur. Ironically, despite its promising beginnings, the state of affairs prevailing in the case at the point which has just been discussed (where 'silence' reigned both within the family and the professional network, each system characterised by poor communication and ultimate splitting and fragmentation) conforms to what Reder *et al.* (1993) describe as the 'mirroring' process whereby relationships on one side are unwittingly acted out by members of the other.

The remaining section of this chapter will focus on two further aspects of long-term work; the use of authority by child protection workers, and the criteria that were used to justify the termination of work in certain cases.

Risk management, the use of authority and parental co-operation

Parton *et al.* (1997) observed that ongoing work in child protection cases largely consists of 'risk management'. By this they meant that work is focused on very specific aspects of family life, those that are perceived as an immediate or potential threat, and concern themselves very little with wider social disadvantage and misfortune. To a certain extent, the same notion is reflected here in this study, in the work done with clients in the allocated cases. Although the range of interventions was reasonably broad, the emphasis was on parenting behaviours and lifestyle change to minimise the potential for the same 'concerns' to arise again. For example, attempts were made to help a neglectful mother achieve a more 'responsible' attitude to her children. They were slow to take effect though there was a slight improvement, according to the social worker:

> I suspect that she would probably think twice before leaving them for lengthy periods at least… She is still rather casual, one of the times I went to see her the older child was minding the other two.

But the social worker's aspirations towards helping the mother in this case deal with other aspects of her life were less productive:

> The reality is that I haven't been that successful in getting her to respond or see a need for much change. So the role has been very limited, not very productive in other areas, other than having some controls.

The social worker for the mother who had a former violent partner had perceived some progress, though he took a somewhat guarded view of it:

> she is saying that everything is fine, she is getting on with her life, she is feeling very positive about everything, she is delighted she went to the refuge, it has helped her an awful lot, she's happy to stay there till the next case conference, she will be planning on moving on then, she'll get herself a flat, and it's grand. And in a sense I have a feeling that this is as far as we're probably going to get. I have this awful feeling that it will really be left there with people not really understanding what has been happening to [the mother] over the years. And maybe [she] herself not understanding what has happened to her, and that she may get herself into a tangle again, depending on what circumstances she meets down the road and then she might not…that sort of thing and I am not sure that we are going to get much further really…

Two issues stand out here. One is the focus on parental behaviours per se, rather than the specific manner in which the behaviours deemed to be problematic impacted on the current welfare and safety of the individual children in the family. It is very apparent that practice was parent rather than child centred, and that it focused on a modern ideal of acceptable parenthood or maternity, an issue dealt with in more depth in the final chapter. This is a theme that has recurred in research over the past decade (Thorpe 1994; Farmer and Owen 1995; Thoburn et al. 1995; Parton et al. 1997). Efforts to re-focus and reclaim the child in child protection have been concretised in the assessment framework adopted in England and Wales in 2000 (Department of Health [UK] 2000) but at this stage no formal evaluation of its operation has been conducted.

The second issue highlighted in the foregoing data is the degree of compromise that is commonly applied to professional aspirations of effecting change in parental behaviour. The model, or 'wheel' of change conceptualised by Prochaska and Di Climenti (1982)[2] and extensively detailed in the material that accompanies the new UK assessment framework (Horwath and Morrison 2001) traces a trajectory from pre-contemplation to maintenance of new behaviour. However, many of the parents in this case study seemed to lack commitment to change, which in terms of the model, means that they remained in moderately compliant pre-contemplation. This was despite the interventions and sometimes the threats, of statutory social workers. Again, this illustrates the way that taken-for-granted theories about child protection work do not sit comfortably with the reality of day-to-day practice.

Effectiveness in child protection work is a very difficult concept to rate in research, as in a context of constantly shifting aims and variables, it is not always clear whose needs or whose objectives are being met (Cheetham et al. 1992, MacDonald 2001). On examination of the cases, it appears that certain common factors operated to modify the original arrangements that had been set up. In particular, a sort of triangular alliance seemed to exist between the authority that the social worker chose to use, the relationship that was forged with the families, and the level of co-operation between them. Both the management of the work and the different outcomes of each case appeared to depend in large degree on the way these three elements interacted. In most of the cases, a kind of bargaining process appeared to evolve, where the balance between control by the social workers and co-operation of the families was mediated by the relationships they shared, again supporting Wise's (1989) notion that 'clear solutions' are rarely applicable.

Corby (1987), in a study completed in the early 1980s in the UK, found that social workers were uncomfortable with the authoritative role they carried as statutory child protection workers, and had to make compromises between their 'caring' and 'controlling' roles, which influenced the way they dealt with clients in certain situations. Throughout the 1990s in the UK, literature on child protection would indicate that the child protection system became far more regulatory of families, though subject to the reins of public backlash from time to time (Parton 1991; Howe 1992; Parton *et al.* 1997) and that different paradigms operated in an almost parallel fashion (Fox Harding 1997; Rodger 1996). In Ireland, a less reflexive culture operated and the family's strong traditional and constitutional position continued to dominate practices throughout the same period (Department of Health 1993; Ferguson 1994; Buckley *et al.* 1997). Chapters Two and Three of this study have shown how social workers were very sensitive to family privacy in their response to child abuse allegations. However, it did appear that when investigations had turned into 'cases' and practitioners were involved over a longer term, they assumed their authoritative roles, if not comfortably, with a certain doggedness. One social worker described how she disliked the role she was forced to assume:

> Terrible stuff…it was very much a policing role that I took on… I didn't want it to be like that initially but that's what it was… It's terrible to be involved in a family in that sort of situation, I don't really think anybody has the right to be going along telling people what they should do…

She was prepared to overcome her inhibitions about 'telling people what they should do', however, when the protection of children was at issue:

> That's why I did it…it's not particularly comfortable… I would have preferred if the family had in some way opened up and I could have been there in a more positive way… The role I am portraying is the checker upper and the big stick really…that's what I am.

Another worker expressed discomfort with the 'monitoring' role she had to play which she described as 'not the way one would like to see oneself'. While she would have liked to achieve different levels of work with her client, she felt the only 'hold' she had over her was her statutory authority:

> I worked on the premise that because I was there in a statutory role, I put it to her how she could best organise things and act to get me off her back, on that kind of basis.

The least experienced and most recently qualified social worker felt that the use of authority needed to be balanced with sensitivity, but was more honest in the long run: 'I don't come into any case in a heavy-handed way, but I'd let clients know where I'd be coming from ... I have a specific role and concern'. He described his initial approach to an investigation of suspected child neglect:

> I was very directive if you like... I think there was no point in going along saying we were interested in building relationships or concerned about the children, because what reason would we have for concerns...unless we had something to go on... I made that very clear to [the mother], and I think she appreciated it, and I asked her...did she know what that meant, and she said that she did, that she had been in contact with social workers in the other area when she lived there, and I said basically it was to do with concerns over the children being left alone and I said I would be in contact with the public health nurse and the school and was that all right with her, so she agreed with that and she offered me a tea and a cigarette. That was the start, I suppose, of a working relationship.

These findings highlight a number of issues in relation to the focus of the work, the context of the work, and the high measure of control exercised by clients of the service. First, it was very clear in these cases that the primary focus of the work was related to the child protection concerns that had brought the services into contact with the family in the first place. There was evidence to show that the work was relatively achievable, as long as the parents, who were mostly mothers, accepted the need if not the reason for intervention. One of the workers attributed the ease he experienced with his authoritative role to the attitude of the particular mother:

> Because she accepts it... I mean this is one of the things, she is at the point where she's accepting the roles, she's not passive by any means, she's extremely assertive and if she doesn't agree with something, she'll say she doesn't agree with something, but she engages in an adult rational sort of a way, you don't get sort of abuse or irrationality or any of that, so I feel comfortable in that situation and she's listening to what you're saying as well, although she might disagree with it she listens...

But not all service users were as amenable. The difficulties the social workers experienced in carrying out the 'heavy' end of their work was exacerbated at times by the context of some of their relationships with families which were underpinned by tension and lack of trust. For example, one social worker described her relationship with a father as follows:

> I mean he would have much preferred if I had died and gone off the face of the earth rather than be going around at all you know, he's very suspicious... I might find out things, like that he was drinking or wasn't using his money efficiently... He would have been happy enough without me there...

These findings are in keeping with Parton et al.'s (1997, p.182) observation that rejection of the 'restricted repertoire' of services on offer from the child protection system is widespread, and that they are likely to be refused because of the stigma attached. For example, the social worker for a mother with an alcohol problem described her as 'someone who just does not want to become engaged with social workers', nor was he having much success engaging her son, who 'expressed his distaste of social workers calling to the school'. Parton et al. (1997) argue that, for the most part, arrangements regarding the reception of services are reluctantly 'negotiated' by the families rather than accepted.

In the light of these findings, it was hardly surprising to discover that the most crucial variable that mediated between the other elements of child protection work was the degree of co-operation that existed between the families and the social workers. This determined not only the quality and level of work, but also the ultimate disposal of the case. In certain instances, where the risks had been about neglect of children, the parents had effectively controlled the level of intervention by their own availability to the social workers. In two separate cases, there were long gaps between contacts. This was because the parents, mothers in both instances, had been out or not answered the door when social workers had called on numerous occasions, often by written appointment. One child sexual abuse case was closed very early because of lack of response from the family. The assessment had not been completed, but the child was considered to have been adequately protected, as the alleged abuse was extra-familial. A number of other cases were about to be closed at the end of the study period, not because the 'child abuse' concerns had abated, but because the clients were no longer interested in working with the statutory system. One of the social workers described a mother's attitude in one case:

> Throughout my involvement with the [family], [the mother] would only move with you to facilitate her own agenda… Neither of them are open to social work in the sense of trying to work through the issues of their relationship and trying to resolve them in a way that will not affect the children, and I'm talking about emotionally.

He felt that there were still concerns about emotional abuse, and also the mental health of the mother, but planned to close the case: 'Because I feel there's clear evidence to show that [the mother] is not prepared to take up the services…in a constructive way'. At the end of the fieldwork period, five months after taking up the case, the social worker in a case of neglect where children were often left unsupervised, concluded that there was little more she could do. This was despite her concerns about the safety of the children who were aged one, four and nine years:

> The most recent one being that I called one evening and found the three children down in the courtyard… This would be at about seven o'clock…and the mother was missing… I would continue to feel concerns about the quality of care really… She has never really been open to help…so I am pessimistic about being able to continue with the family really in any kind of productive, or possibly productive way… I would be thinking of closing it.

A mother in a different case was 'not prepared to engage with the services' either, according to her social worker. He lost contact with her two months after his initial involvement in the case:

> Most weeks I have made attempts and she's never there. And she has not... I have made appointments down here and there has been no response to the notes I have left.

The social worker had previously expressed concerns about the mother's need for support in the foreseeable future. Her son had previously spent a period in care because of her problem alcohol consumption and there were rumours that she was drinking again. However, the mother's lack of availability caused him to terminate his efforts to see her and her son, believing that 'that case can be closed unless some other social worker can have a more imaginative way of engaging with [her]'.

The workers in the above cases had intermittent contact with the children's schools, or had some other way of indirectly monitoring the different situations. They almost all saw some signs of improvement: one mother had got a new flat, so that her accommodation problems had eased; another 'may have gained from being in the refuge... in terms of just looking at some of the issues and looking at where her life was going'. A neglectful parent was getting her children to school more often and there were less complaints about her leaving them unattended for such long periods. However, the main reason for ceasing direct contact in many of these cases was not the level of progress that had been made, but the poor level of co-operation between the families and the social workers, and the disengagement of the parents.

This is an important point when the nature of the work and the responsibility of workers are considered, because more than anything else, it illustrates the limits of the child protection discourse. As Howe (1992, p.506) argues, in the context of proceduralised and bureaucratised agency responses to child abuse, 'not all the actors in the situation have so readily accepted their role and what is expected of them'. The 'discretion' of parents, who according to Howe, remain the 'jokers' in the pack, 'continues to challenge the solutions and may even challenge the question' (p.506). These findings also reflect the concept of 'closure' identified by Reder et al. (1993, p.99), which they describe as: 'an issue about control with parents feeling that they were in precarious control of their lives and that outsiders were unwelcome intruders who would further undermine them'. Reder *et al.* suggest that in many of these cases, past histories illustrated control conflicts between the families and authorities. Similarly, the majority of the cases in this study which were 'about to be closed' had been open and closed in the past and most had records of poor co-operation.

Conclusion

This chapter has offered further examples of the unique way in which practitioners made sense of their work in an uncertain context, using a case example to depict its complex and dynamic nature. The active, rather than passive, involvement of both professionals and families became visible in terms of the political and personal manoeuvres used by the social workers around decisions to take on cases for longer term work, and the strategies used by families to either accommodate social work intervention or keep the workers at a distance.

It also became clear that although cases were prioritised on the basis of child abuse risks, over time the perceived hazards in the different situations began to appear less threatening, and the overall image of the work became much less dramatic. What became more obvious was that once cases survived the child abuse filter, they were available for a range of interventions, but the necessary prerequisite for agency 'recognition' in the form of allocation was conformity to a minimum threshold of child maltreatment. Most decision-making was therefore made with reference to this framework. Workers tended to account for their activities through a colloquial or 'contingent repertoire' rather than reflect on them theoretically, relying on experience and collegial support to guide them. One of the elements of the child protection process which became more visible as the case careers developed was the crucial balance between the authority of the social workers and the co-operation of the families, which was often mediated by the type of relationship which existed between them. While social workers experienced a universal discomfort with the level of power that both they and their clients acknowledged, they did appear to accept their responsibilities in that regard. However, there was further affirmation that most of their attentions were directed towards mothers, and theoretical propositions about avoidance and mitigation of fathers were again confirmed.

Evidence of the strength of interactional processes in child protection situations was again manifested; inter-agency and inter-professional issues continued to impact on the work, most marked by professional entrenchment within various positions and paradigms. Problems around communication became even more embedded, and the futility of assuming mutual collaborative commitment to work between agencies and disciplines in the longer term became obvious. Another interesting process began to dominate practice, however, in a very decisive fashion: parental co-operation, or lack of it. The weakness in the child protection discourse began to manifest itself when it became clear that not only were practitioners active in manipulating the system to suit particular situations, but that parents could be extremely powerful in both controlling the level and quality of intervention, and ultimately in terminating contact alto- gether, irrespective of the perceived progress made, or the existing situa- tion with regard to the protection and welfare of the children.

It is timely therefore to turn to an examination of parental perspectives on the child protection system, an area that has received little attention in Irish research. The next chapter describes the experiences of a sample of parents, mostly mothers, whose children were the subject of professional concern and who agreed to talk to me about what it was like for them.

Endnotes

1   A two day training course on the principles of 'brief therapy' had recently been attended by some members of the team, including the two workers who attempted to incorporate it into their work practice.

2   Prochaska and Di Climenti's (1982) wheel of change describes a process characterised by five stages: contemplation, determination, action, main- tenance and lapse. The process is preceded by the stage of pre-contemplation and can include a stage of relapse.

Chapter Six

The Parents' Perspectives

Introduction

So far, this book has demonstrated the dynamic elements of child protection work, those which render it less predictable, resolvable, and less amenable to management and prescription than is assumed in the official discourse. This chapter now moves on to consider a frequently ignored dimension of the child protection system, the parents whose children have been the subject of 'child abuse' concerns. Within the qualitative paradigm adopted by this research, allowance is made for what Trinder (1996, p.239) refers to as the 'de-centring of the expert' so that the voices of other participants can move 'centre stage'. By this means the parents can, through their accounts or stories, join in the research process itself.

The previous chapter has illustrated the pivotal position of parents in determining the activities of professional practitioners, and the futility of efforts to pursue certain interventions without their co-operation. This chapter now explains, through the voices of the parents, how the experience of being service users impacts on them. As in previous chapters, a number of case examples will be used to illustrate a wide range of issues, but the M case will again dominate, mainly this time through the perspective of Mrs M.

The most recent child protection guidance published in Ireland (Department of Health and Children 1999), while avoiding the term 'partnership', emphasises the value in involving parents as much as possible in the child protection process. Likewise, the Children Act 2001 lays considerable emphasis on both parental involvement and parental responsibility.

However, policies and procedures in operation at the time this fieldwork was conducted paid little regard to the perspectives of parents. The 1999 guidelines reflected research findings in Ireland and the UK regarding the strong links between parental involvement and positive outcomes in child protection (Buckley *et al.* 1997; Thoburn *et al.* 1995; Cleaver and Freeman 1995).

On the other hand, Corby *et al.* (1996) and Bell (2000) have demonstrated that the notion of working together with parents is far more restricted and problematic than is recognised in official guidelines and current research. There was no perceptible policy on parental participation in Ballyowen at the time this study was carried out. It was not a concept which greatly occupied the professionals, though the data presented in Chapter Three illustrate the concerns experienced by practitioners about parents' rights to know that their names were on 'lists' in relation to notifications being made about them, and Chapter Four reflects the tendency of professionals to advocate greater parental participation in child protection conferences. It would have been invidious, however, for this study to claim that it had explored the level of partnership with parents as there was really no visible aspiration to achieve this at the time. This chapter seeks instead to represent the perspectives of a number of parents involved in the child protection system, and the ways in which they experienced it. It is essentially more concerned with identifying the key factors inherent in relationships between professionals and clients that impact on the nature and quality of child protection work carried out.

The sample of parents interviewed for this phase of the research was not chosen to represent the entire cohort of service users included in the study. Instead, it was limited to the cases that had remained 'open' to the end of the fieldwork, and those on which child protection conferences had been held. These two groups overlapped, with the exception of two cases, where conferences had been held but no further action taken. In the open cases, the interviews with parents were arranged through the social workers. I contacted the parents in the two closed cases by letter. Where there were two parents involved, I asked to speak to them both. In all, 14 parents were interviewed, from 11 out of a possible 19 families. Of the remainder, some refused, and others offered appointments but were not at home when I called, which I interpreted as a change of mind. I interviewed ten mothers, and four fathers, three of whom were separated from their families. In one case where I interviewed the father, the mother was unwilling to speak to me. In two other instances, I had arranged to meet both parents, but in the event only the mothers were available. The interviews took place during the last month of the fieldwork period, in the family homes.

In examining the experiences of parents in the child protection system, it is important to differentiate between those who were regarded as responsible for the abuse, and those whose children were allegedly abused by others, inside and outside their families. Their 'operational perspectives' (Cleaver and Freeman 1995) were considerably influenced according to whether or not they believed that culpability was being ascribed to them. As illustrated in chapters Three and Five, the child protection investigations and interventions tended to focus on mothers, even when the incident that triggered off the concern had allegedly been perpetuated by their husbands or partners. Chapter Three also demonstrated that a major constituent of the child protection assessment was the adjudication of the mother's ability to protect the child or children from further harm. This practice had been applied in relation to the sample families that featured at this stage of the study, with one exception where the mother was the principal alleged perpetrator and the father was the focus of intervention. He was considered more reasonable, and was more available to the worker involved, as the mother was frequently under the influence of alcohol, or out of the home.

The data gathered from interviews with the parents could be clustered in the following ways:

- first, parents' attitude to the initial allegations, and the way they experienced the investigation and initial contact with the board
- second, their views on the nature of service offered to them

- third, the type of relationships that existed between themselves and the social workers, and how this impacted on them

- fourth, their own perceptions of how their needs were understood and met, and how they conceptualised the help that they received.

Parents' understanding of child abuse and perceptions of their own parenting

There were obvious links between the sources of referral, the alleged 'culpability' of the parents and the ways in which the families viewed their contact with the social services. In six of the fourteen cases featured in this chapter, the parents believed that their children were, or had been, at risk at the time of the initial referral and investigation. These included the four who had instigated the contact, and the two families whose children had first disclosed abuse at their schools. For example, in one case a father conceded that his wife's drinking was putting his family's safety in jeopardy, though he himself had not initiated a request for help:

> The kids were under pressure like, and in danger… The house could have been burnt…anything could have happened, it was a very dangerous kind of situation to be in.

In another case, a mother had sought help because she was desperately worried about her son who was 15 at the time:

> He would go off the deep end with the tablets… He would either disappear and not come in at all or he would come in at six o'clock in the morning… He wouldn't tell me who he was with, where he was or what he was doing… I was waiting for the Gardaí to call to say he was either in the [river] or he was after being beaten up and was in some hospital or other.

Two of the families featuring in this phase of the research had been referred because of sexual abuse. They had at the time indicated a level of awareness regarding the abusive nature of what had happened. One family referred themselves for 'support, advice and counselling' after an adult neighbour had allegedly sexually abused their three-year-old child. In another case, the mother was 'devastated and shocked' when she discovered her husband's sexual abuse of their children, but did not appear to doubt the seriousness of it.

On the other hand, some parents who were referred by other persons or agencies were in some cases less inclined to acknowledge the nature or degree of the maltreatment being suggested, their construction of 'child abuse' bearing little resemblance to that which they felt was operated by the social workers. For example, a lone mother who had been reported for leaving her two and four-year-old children alone in their flat, insisted that she was doing nothing wrong:

> I often leave them when I go over to the shop… to me…I don't think there's anything wrong with that… I make them sit down, make sure the fire and the kettle is plugged out… It's very hard for me to manage, with two kids, if it's lashing rain, to drag them across the road and all, and get them soaking wet… rather than just flying over and coming straight back.

She disputed the gravity of what she had done, comparing it with the type of behaviour which she *would* deem unacceptable: 'abusing, slapping and leaving marks or anything…kicking the child, or neglecting or not feeding the child'. 'Leaving' children for long periods was, however, generally considered by the parents interviewed to be a dangerous practice, as was over parentification (i.e. expecting young children to carry adult or parental responsibilities) of young children. One of the mothers interviewed believed such behaviour to be potentially far worse than the 'smacking' she employed as means of discipline with her own children:

> Like a 12-year-old to look after three young kids… It's he that's being neglected and abused…that's my definition of abuse…there's also physical abuse as well… I smack the older boy, I don't deny it… I think he needs to be smacked sometimes to actually control him…

But smacking, in her mind, was infinitely less harmful than:

> …telling the children that they are stupid, or 'Don't be ridiculous…' I don't think they should be made feel like that… I think that's really cruel. Neglect is not giving your children attention, not playing with them, quality time, there's all different types of neglect…not watching your children.

A lone mother who was referred to the Health Board because she was 'under pressure' insisted that her children were 'never, never' at risk in her care, and another who was referred after she and her child were injured in a physical assault by her former partner, acknowledged that she had problems with 'the drinking, and more or less the baby's father' but denied any shortcomings in the quality of her parenting: 'I'm not saying everything I did was right, but I'm not the worst, you know what I mean... There are people five times worse who get away...'.

These constructions, or otherwise, of 'abuse' were offered by mothers who had been reported to social services, and interviewed by social workers in relation to concerns which the mothers themselves did not believe to constitute inadequate care, or maltreatment. The comparisons they made between their own 'misdemeanours' and 'real' child abuse indicated the level of sense-making that they applied in their own personal environments. As Cleaver and Freeman (1995, p.120) assert: 'In the realm of perception and operational perspectives, much depends on the meaning attributed to "abuse" in different situations and by different families.' Discrepancy in perceptions can, suggest Cleaver and Freeman, determine the 'consistency and durability' of parents' operational perspectives. Such a pattern, as the case examples have shown, was replicated in this study.

Parents' experience of the initial child abuse investigation

Thoburn *et al.* (1995) describe how, in their study, parents expressed mixed reactions to the investigative process, whether they were implicated in the alleged abuse or not. In this study, views were equally mixed in relation to the investigative process, but the variable of whether parents were implicated or not did appear to be important, as did the amount of support and practical help that followed the investigation. Those parents who referred *themselves* to the social work service were reconciled to the process of the investigation, and in some instances, quite positive about it. One self-referring mother claimed she had found it a useful experience: 'very good, very helpful, I actually learned a lot from them'. Another self-referring mother who had previously been reported to the Health Board by a professional but this time made the contact herself, was positive about the response she got:

> This time around I found them helpful…and I have to say it was more open, I understood things better… Possibly I have a better relationship with the Health Board, this time, because I started it… I was actually availing of the services, and they were helping me out like…

In a study of professional interventions in child sexual abuse, Sharland *et al.* (1996, p.76) describe the emotional responses of parents on the discovery of sexual abuse of their children, and name the most overwhelming initial feelings as: 'shock, guilt and a profound sense of grief and loss'. CM's mother fitted this template, and found it very difficult to come to terms with what the social workers who first broke the news to her had to say. Her husband, the alleged perpetrator, was more resigned, and had no criticisms of the investigation:

> I thought it was handled well, I was called to the house and told of the claims… [of what] I had done… It's not their fault that the child didn't come and tell me…

The father whose daughter had complained about the effects of her mother's drinking was satisfied with the way the social worker approached him: 'It wasn't over the top, no, the individual call to us was very low profile, you could say. She was out to help us any way she could'.

The mother who was referred by the Children's Hospital after her child got injured in the 'crossfire' of an exchange between herself and her former partner, was happy enough with the investigation, because in her own view she was not the guilty party. Two lone mothers who had been reported by other persons or agencies for, in the first case, alleged neglect and emotional abuse, and in the second, alleged sexual and physical abuse, were annoyed at the accusations that had been levelled against them, but actually found the investigative process quite supportive, and worthwhile. They both accepted the need for follow up of child abuse allegations. As one of them acknowledged:

> They have to be careful and if they get a report they have to check it out… I can understand why they do it, because there's kids, and parents go out and they're left there for hours on their own.

While she felt the investigation was unjustified in her own case, she was ultimately grateful that her problems got an airing:

There's times I could cry out for help and nobody would know... In a way it was a godsend like...it all came flooding out...everything that was wrong, I was saying it was all right when really it wasn't... So I'm not saying they should ignore us, like.

The other mother also spoke of the positive outcome of the investigation in her situation:

Well, a good thing has come out of it... He sees that nothing is wrong with [her daughter], and he's there for another reason as well, to help me with financial support, that's what he said, if I have any money worries. In a sense it was a horrible thing to happen, at the beginning, but...out of something bad...something good...

Both of these mothers were grateful for the practical support with finance and with the management of their children that they received following the initial investigation, and this appeared to mitigate their initial annoyance at the intrusion into their lives. However, a mother who had been anonymously reported for neglect, emotional abuse and physical abuse by a neighbour and then exonerated, had no social work contact or intervention following her interview with the duty social worker. Her memory of the occasion was very unpleasant and reflected Cleaver and Freeman's (1995, p.83) conception of the 'trapped' feeling experienced by parents during the 'initial confrontation', when they felt that everything they said or did was given a hostile interpretation. She described what it was like for her:

I got a letter... I couldn't make out what was going on and I read it again, and it just stated that there had been allegations made...that whole evening I was just sitting here just wondering... So we went in and [the social worker] saw us, and it started off with an allegation that I left the children unattended for periods of up to a few hours... My first reaction was actually to laugh...and then it went on and I realised, no misunderstanding here, somebody has said something and it's quite firm what they have said... It upset me, and then the next thing that was said was that I hit the children, like abused the children physically... That's when I felt actually really intimidated.

I just couldn't think... We wanted to know who it was, and then we couldn't... What made me so angry was the fact that the person was protected, and I felt under suspicion... They spoke to my GP... I didn't even know they had done that, and that's when I really felt scared.

Although she said the social worker was 'very nice' to her, and very 'tactful' she recalled hearing the allegations in a very stark way:

> ...leaving your children for four hours, beating your children, locking them up... He was very nice when he said those things, he didn't make them sound like that at all, but that was the way I heard them...beating, leaving, neglecting...

During the interview, during which the parents had emphatically denied the allegations, the social worker had told both parents that he 'didn't see any problem here' and didn't need to see them again. Nonetheless, the whole process had a profound effect on the mother, particularly the notion that one of her neighbours had reported her. She had been previously treated for depression and though she had fully recovered, she began to feel very low again after the interview:

> I could feel myself immediately going back... It was like the tidal wave that I had felt...before... I was in a very bad state... I became obsessed... I didn't want the children near me, I was saying no...better keep them away... This was up to weeks afterwards, I was...constantly crying.

In this case, the social worker had been responding to what seemed like very serious allegations of neglect made by a neighbour, who reported that the mother was leaving her children for periods of time, and emotionally and physically abusing them on other occasions. Problems about health and relationships within the family had been mentioned, but they had been overshadowed by the dominance of the 'child abuse' elements in the referral. The report had been notified to the Director, a child protection conference had endorsed the need for an investigative interview where these allegations could be put to the mother, and an explanation sought. Within these parameters (by which I mean responding to an allegation, a notification and conference recommendations), it is difficult to see how an investigation could have been managed more sensitively. Had it been referred some other way, perhaps as a concern for the stress that this mother was suffering, it may have been possible to make a more proactive, and less forensic response, perhaps mediated through a different professional. However, within a discourse that judges child care concerns only in terms of the risks they present, and given the practice norms which were operating at the time, it is unlikely that it would have received any follow up at all unless it was framed as 'child abuse/neglect'.

It appears from these findings that parents rated 'child abuse' in varying ways, and in several instances those who were themselves alleged to have abused or neglected their children had difficulty reconciling the need for a child protection investigation with their own versions of 'good enough' parenting. In general, the experience of being investigated was very traumatic for some parents, though when it led to the provision of support, they were more conciliatory about it.

Parents' views on the child protection system

There was no specific agency policy operating in Ballyowen on 'partnership' with parents at the time of the study, and practice varied as to whether or not parents were actually told that a complaint had been made about them, or if initial inquiries were made about them to public health nurses or other professionals. Despite this inconsistency, some of the parents who were interviewed found the social workers quite 'open'. However, this was not a universal experience; one of the mothers who had been referred by a treatment service, said she was never told that social services had been contacted about her. Another mother was shocked that her general practitioner and the public health nurse had been asked for their opinions of her parenting skills, and that a child protection conference had been held without her knowledge. In other respects, difficulty was experienced by some parents in accessing information. For example, Mrs M tried to find out how her husband was progressing in therapy:

> I phoned [the therapist] once to see how he was doing and he wasn't...he didn't give me any encouragement to want to see him like... He just said, 'Oh I can't say'... And like they never wanted to meet me... I kind of wasn't given any encouragement to meet them or they never suggested... I mean like...meet them if there was something that I could do that would be helpful or whatever, but there was nothing...no reaction. Ok, I know what they talk about is confidential... I don't want to know what

he's talking about, I want to know what progress he's making... I just think that... I'm entitled to that.

Similar findings about poor communication and parents' perceptions that information was being concealed from them were reported in studies by Farmer and Owen (1995) and Thoburn *et al.* (1995). Yet as Cleaver and Freeman (1995, p.87) have pointed out, one of the rare ways in which interactions of professionals and parents may be 'smoothed' in such a conflicted context is by the sharing of information, which clearly did not happen in the case mentioned above.

Parental participation in child protection conferences

Some parents felt that being able to attend child protection conferences might have given them access to more information that they felt they were not getting otherwise. As explained in Chapter Four, it was not the policy in Ballyowen to invite parents to participate in full child protection conference discussions. With one exception, the parents whom I interviewed would have appreciated the opportunity to attend the conferences held to discuss their situations. The mother who said she would not have wanted to be there claimed that she would have been 'aggravated', and 'would probably have torn the head off somebody'. However, her view was not shared by the other parents. Another mother expressed her view as follows:

> I would have liked to know what was going on with the future of my child, because after all she is my daughter, I'm the one that brought her into the world, I've reared her, I'm the one that has brought her up so far on my own... So she is part of me, she is my flesh and blood... I have a right to know what is going on... I'd like to know what they're going to decide.

Likewise, the mother of a 15-year-old boy would have found it a useful experience to attend:

> I would have liked to know what was going on actually, what they thought, and where they would see it going... I would have liked to have everybody there together and sort of... What do you think is the outcome, or what do you see is down the road for us... Do you know what I mean?

A couple who had sought a service because their three-year-old had been abused by a neighbour had, in their own words, 'grown cynical of the system' prior to the child protection conference. They considered that they could perhaps have found out what was going on about the police investigation of the case:

> If it would have meant that there would have been some information or some decisions that we could have got out of the people involved... To ask questions, to which maybe we could have got better answers.

Mrs M blamed her exclusion from conferences upon her failure to understand that she should not have allowed her husband back into the family home. Her response is very illustrative of the difficulties frequently experienced by mothers in coming to terms with their children's abuse by a partner (Hooper 1992):

> I firmly believe if I had been at that I would have understood an awful lot more... I was just brought in at the end, and told, no contact, end of story like. I mean...nothing. Everything was over, everything was decided. I wasn't able to give a view of what I thought or anything, it was over, it was decided and that was it, and I was just being brought in to be told, which I didn't think was right... I think I should have been there when everyone else was there, and while they were discussing it...so as I would know what they were discussing... I think I would have learned a lot and understood a lot more, and I would have understood the seriousness of having my husband out of the house... It was after that that he came back, and I think in many ways... I don't know, but I feel maybe I was retaliating against them, because I felt they shut me out... I do honestly believe that if I had been at that case conference I would have seen it, because naturally they would have been talking about everything and I would have had to... I can't have been that stupid that I wouldn't have picked up a certain amount... It would have been hard and I would have been very upset... It certainly would have been worth it, no matter what I would have went through, no matter what hurt or upset I would have felt, it still would have been worth it, and I think that at the end of the day, I would have seen things better.

The mother of two small children, reported for alleged emotional and physical abuse, also felt that her own presence at the case conference would have 'let them know' what she did or did not want in terms of a service. In her view, the decision to allocate a family support worker to her was unnecessary:

> A few people came here, but it wasn't what I wanted... I told [the referring social worker] I didn't need anybody but they said even somebody to talk to...and I felt like... God, I wish all these people would go away, because there's too many of them, and I don't need all this.

The mother reported for physically abusing her children and leaving them unsupervised while she was out said she would have found it difficult to sit through a child protection conference about herself and her family, but would also have tolerated the discomfort for the sake of being present:

> I would have been very embarrassed...but I think, yes, I think you should hear what people are saying...not behind your back... I think that while they are sitting around a table, discussing a case, they should have brought you in... Then to say 'We're a team of social workers or whatever and we're going to sit down and we're going to discuss what we have heard and we'd like you to hear the evidence as well'.

These findings replicate those of Farmer and Owen (1995) and Thoburn *et al.* (1995), illustrating that contrary to the views of professionals quoted in Chapter Three, parents were willing to display more courage than the practitioners when it came to undertaking a potentially threatening experience.

Parents' criticisms of the child protection service

Most parents found specific aspects of the service helpful, an issue that will be developed later, but some strong criticisms were voiced by a number of them. For example, the value of holding child protection conferences was, in the view of some parents, overrated. One of the mothers believed that nothing useful had emanated from the meeting on their situation, despite the time and trouble involved in setting it up:

> The most amazing thing... There didn't seem to be any decision or anything implemented from that...whatsoever, I mean... It must have been reasonably complicated to organise something with people...to get the general practitioner and all these people to find a day that is mutually suitable and to bring all of these people for what is actually the

outcome…in our mind absolutely nil… There was nothing…nothing out of it…

She was also critical of the 'difficulty of dealing with people who weren't handling it properly':

> This is going to sound extremely critical, what I found was that your first priority when something like that happens is to come to terms with it so that you can help your child. Because what happened was that there was added pain and difficulty because of the deficiency of the system… What had happened was bad enough, but was not helped by the way people who are skilled or whatever cope with this.

Hooper (1992) observed that the involvement of agencies at the initial stages of intra-familial child sexual abuse investigation was not always followed up with support in the aftermath, and women were often left on their own coping with their own and their children's feelings. The same trend appeared in this study; for example, Mrs M was critical of the lack of treatment and support her family were given:

> I was told from the very beginning that top priority was that [the child] was to go into counselling and I was to go into counselling. And nothing has happened for any of us… And now, given…now…at this precise moment, I think that there should have been some kind of counselling… I definitely think it could be dealt with differently… The follow up is not good… They are not giving the proper help to people.

The mother who suffered a recurrence of depression after a child abuse allegation was made about her felt she needed help after being confronted with the report and was critical of the fact that none was offered by the social worker:

> Why didn't they have somebody here? Why didn't they say to somebody, just go up and talk her through what we have done… I would hate to think of somebody else like me, and I'm sure it has happened, just being landed and not being forewarned about… Don't expect too much back-up, because they haven't really got time for the counselling…

Likewise, the mother whose young child had been abused by an adult neighbour said that she and her family had 'no sense of support or solidarity':

It remained totally vague… And nobody said 'We'll organise therapy for your daughter, and here is the name of somebody and here is how it can be done…' and whatever…or 'The parents themselves might need counselling…' Nothing was done.

She had noted that the Health Board was mainly concerned with the protection of children:

She [the social worker] said 'For us, the priority is the protection of children and in your case the child is living with you so she is not at risk, therefore it's not really that important'… From that point of view, it was presented in that kind of way.

An estranged husband who had been accused of sexually abusing his children and later exonerated, was very frustrated at how little attention the Health Board was paying to his own complaints about his wife's inadequate parenting skills. He had concluded that the Health Board was only interested in sexual abuse:

The response was very slow…nobody ever heard my calling about the neglect of the children. [The social worker] still isn't responding in the way I thought people should respond… It's all very lackadaisical you know, it's very long process… All he [did] was look after the allegations of child sexual abuse… If there was no child sexual abuse going on, nothing else mattered, you know.

Relationships between parents and social workers

Despite the negativity expressed by some of the parents, the majority of them had what seemed like good relationships with their social workers, and commented positively when they felt they had been treated fairly, or where they liked or trusted the individual practitioners. As one of them put it:

[The social worker] is wonderful, he has a great sense of humour… I get on with him. I think it's how you perceive the social worker … if you like the person, that helps a hell of a lot… I can be totally honest with him, and sit down and say 'I'm not able to handle it'…or 'I am'. If you trust the person and are able to get on with them, that is a lot, because if you are having a huge problem and you feel like you can't trust the person, you can't tell them… They may do something drastic…they might take him off me or they might do this or that... You won't tell them... I mean if I had something that was really bugging me I'd rather sit and wear it on my shoulders than tell anyone if I thought... Do you know what I mean? But if you feel like you can talk to him, if you can open up to your social worker, then that's a hell of a lot, a lot off your chest.

Not all the relationships between social workers and parents were as satisfactory, however, particularly when the workers were associated with bringing the parents 'bad news' at the outset of their involvement. Cleaver and Freeman (1995) suggest that a change of social worker, particularly from the investigating social worker to another, can make a significant difference to parents' 'operational perspectives' of the service. Likewise, Thoburn *et al.* (1995) found that a change of worker could redress the balance with parents who had had previous poor relationships with the agency. This theory was borne out by Mrs M's account of the relationship she had with her first social worker, who had brought her news of her daughter's disclosure of sexual abuse:

I didn't get on with [the social worker], I'm not saying it was her or my fault... It was a bit of both, and I was never happy talking to her, I'd never sat and talked to her... I never felt comfortable...so when anything would happen, I wouldn't phone her. I didn't feel able, confident enough to ring her.

I don't know... I just...never felt comfortable, and if she didn't come I was happy as Larry, but once she was coming I was sick, I was in fear... I dreaded... I'd actually be sick for a day or two before she came. It's probably stupid, but I can't help the way I feel, do you know... That's something in me and I can't help it... I'm not saying one social worker is better than another, I don't mean that, I'm saying I really do think for future cases, if the person is not happy, and I am sure... I think they should suggest changing and see if it works better... I mean, given a certain length of time, I think if something is not progressing, there has to be some kind of change.

Mrs M had viewed her social worker in terms of what Hooper (1992, p.147) describes as 'control functions', a common occurrence with mothers of children who have been sexually abused and feel disempowered both by events and statutory intervention. Hooper argues for the allocation of a separate social worker for mother and children. Mrs

M did not actually get a separate worker as such, but nine months after initial contact the first social worker went on extended sick leave and was replaced. When I interviewed Mrs M, she was much happier with the new worker:

> I find working with [the new social worker] brilliant, and [he] has brought a lot out in me. I mean I have told and talked to [him] more in the last three weeks than I ever did to [the first social worker] in the last nine months… I have told [him] things that happened even years ago that I had buried…that I didn't know… I didn't think it was possible to bury things, I really didn't, so in that in itself I feel very comfortable with him.

> I actually like when he says 'Will you come down?', I like going up to meet him, I actually feel, I suppose it sounds stupid saying enjoy, but I do enjoy it to an extent, because I actually release something… I feel relief.

Non-abusing parents

Mrs M's situation also illustrated the particular position that non-abusing mothers found themselves in when their 'failure to protect' was the issue. Hooper (1992, p.133) argues that the different positions of abusing and non-abusing parents are frequently not considered by social workers, and suggests that in the context of scarce resources 'increased expectations and surveillance of mothers as primary carers' come into play. Hooper also drew attention to the pressures that mothers had to undergo in dealing with children who were traumatised. Mrs M gave graphic examples of how this affected her:

> I mean, I had the kids crying into my face every night looking for him, and I was upset seeing them upset and I was saying, well, what's the harm in him coming for an hour or half an hour and they were happy… I was happy to see them happy and that was it, it kept them going. I worry about the children all the time.

Hooper also outlined the way that the losses involved for mothers, particularly when their partners had perpetrated the abuse, impacted on their ability to come to terms with what had happened. Mrs M had found herself in an emotional turmoil:

> I'm 22 years with him, 17 years married, you don't just switch off loving someone when you have loved them for that length of time. I mean, I feel

> a lot of hatred towards him, I feel very angry, and a lot of things, but deep down I would still love him, you can't get rid of something that's been there for all those years, most of my life... I mean I'm with him since I was 16, so I can't just say 'He's done this, I don't love him'. Love doesn't really work like that. I think there was a lot expected of me. I think I was expected to hate my husband straight away...not love him and not forgive him, which didn't happen. I would have to say I would still forgive him because I would be a forgiving person, and I still love him, but I would be very... In the last three or four weeks I would be very, very angry towards him and very, very hurt.

Hooper further observes how the pain that is experienced by non-abusing mothers is exacerbated by the guilt they feel, a point also made by Sharland *et al.* (1996). Again, this was an issue for Mrs M: 'I always felt everything was very negative, and I always felt everything was my fault.' A mother whose ex-partner had been violent to her also sensed some accusatory attitudes against herself when she and her baby went into the women's refuge:

> When I first went in...the questions I was asked, it was like they thought I had abused... Do you know what I mean? I got the feeling they thought I was sexually abusing him or something, it was the way the questions were directed at you, like do you abuse the child, have you ever abused the child, do you intend to abuse him? When in fact I was not the abuser at all, but I felt like I was being imposed upon these questions and was made to feel I was the one...and I never laid a hand on him.

In addition to the sense of blame that was experienced by these mothers, the notion that they were solely responsible for the welfare and protection of their children was perceived. As the aforementioned mother expressed it: 'If a mother puts her child in care, she doesn't care about her child and so on... But if the father legs it...that's just natural'. A mother accused of physical abuse and neglect pointed out how the allegations were directed at herself, not her and her husband:

> It actually caused friction in my relationship afterwards... We don't argue much about anything, but it has put a strain on us. He would say something like... 'Well, I wasn't accused of anything' and then it puts doubts in my mind, am I a bad parent, do I do things wrong?...

One of the questions that was asked [of the husband] was actually damaging and still damages me… 'Do you ever pop home to make sure that everything is ok?' And I looked, and I thought like… If you just want me to leave the house I'll leave…

Embedded in the notion of mothers' responsibility for the care and protection of their children is the belief that they are 'safer' and better parents, according to one of the fathers interviewed. He was very bitter that even though his wife retracted her accusation that he had sexually abused their children, he was still regarded as guilty, and nobody would pay attention to his own concerns about his wife's care of the children:

The allegations have been disproved and I'm still in the wings, like… I haven't any right to see my child… I'm living on someone else's floor and she's down there wrecking the house and she's abusing them children…it's a joke… She can say 'boo' and no one would question her… Women are getting all the…it's unbelievable… I couldn't believe how isolated you could be.

He blamed what he described as 'the motherhood syndrome' whereby women were generally seen as above reproach.

Parents' perceptions of the power of the child protection system

As already indicated, in some cases parents described an easy relationship with the statutory services, and had the sense that they were being listened to and not being 'told what to do'. There were times, however, for several parents when they became very aware of the power of the local authority in relation to their children and found it quite intimidating. One woman described how she felt when she was asked to wait while the social worker discussed her situation with some colleagues:

I was scared stiff, I thought [the baby] was going to be taken into care, I'll never forget it…the sweat…I was in an awful state. [The baby] was in the hospital, they kept him there for two or three days, and they said to me… 'Go up to see this social worker' … and I went up to him … My nerves were gone, and then he said to me 'It's one o'clock, you are going to have to go off for an hour…' I was in such a panic.

She was particularly annoyed about a false allegation made by a police officer, and felt helpless about it:

> I was very aggravated, even [the social worker] said this, that one of the Gardaí had made a statement about me and then he retracted it and I didn't find out for two weeks after it was retracted... The damage had been done, do you know what I mean, because I felt it had been taken into context and had been used against me, do you know what I mean? That's the way I felt.

Mrs M also felt very powerless in relation to the system, and described how she felt she would have to conform to the expectations of her previous social worker, whom she believed would be taking over the case again:

> It's a very uncomfortable position to be in, and I will...do anything it takes, if I have to get down on my hands and knees to her I'll do it to get my children back, and I'll feel I have to do... If she told me to swing out of those lights now, I'd do it. Just to be on her side, just to do whatever she says.

Likewise, a mother suspected of physical abuse and neglect and later exonerated, was very nervous of what might happen at her interview with the social worker: 'I even was scared, I thought if I say something during the interview will they think it's wrong and are they going to suspect me...' She felt very helpless, particularly in the context of the difficulties she had with her children. One of them had chronic though not life threatening illnesses, and this meant his sleeping and eating patterns were upset. She found the process of caring for him quite exhausting, as she described it: 'I just fumble my way through the day', and resented being criticised:

> I just felt... Who has the right to tell you how you should be? ... I tried my best and if your best isn't good enough, then I'm sorry...but that's a fault...but I have seen parents much worse than me... I don't know why they did it to me, but they did a fair whack... They gave it a fair whack...

This chapter has so far reported on the perceptions of parents in relation to being investigated, their judgements as to whether or not their children received good enough parenting from themselves, their opinion of the efficacy of the child protection system and the processes adopted by it, their relationships with their social workers and the way they felt they were regarded. However, what appeared to be the most crucial aspect of their views of the service, was the degree to which they considered that a mutual understanding had been reached between themselves and the child protection workers involved with them about what kind of supports they might need.

One of the features most commonly shared by the parents I interviewed was their general lack of social support. A minority of them had some contact with their own parents, or siblings who would help out from time to time, but most of them had nobody they could rely on to give them a break, financial help, or assistance with their children. In several cases, this was because their families were from outside the area, but in others, it was because of a particular combination of events that were not unconnected with the reasons for referral. A lone mother commented that her parents had more or less rejected her because they thought her life was chaotic, particularly after she had the second child out of wedlock, and by a different father:

> My family help out...my parents did... But not at the moment, things are on the bad side, I never ever discussed anything with them like I would never sit down and say 'I have this problem' or 'I have that problem', because they would see it like that's you, you're being careless... There was never really much there beforehand but there's nothing there now.

Mrs M had been too ashamed to tell her neighbours or even her family initially, about her husband's sexual abuse of the children. At the time of his interview with me, Mr M was living away from his family but not connected with any service, because he had 'broken the rules' by returning to his family home and had been expelled from the treatment group he had been attending:

> There was only the group and that's gone now... Ok, I have broken the rules and will be punished... I failed...and was thrown out... I hope I have a chance to get back and in the meantime I was hoping he could arrange something with the psychiatrist. I hope that can happen...otherwise I'll be lost.

Mr M's experience reflects Thoburn *et al.*'s (1995) observation that social workers in child protection do not prioritise help and support for alleged abusers, particularly sexual abusers who have left the family home.

Another mother who had initiated contact with the Health Board after her ex-husband had severely beaten her son, described how little support she was offered by him:

> He has access to the kids on Sundays, that's as far as it goes, he gives me a few bob but he doesn't want to know... Since [son] ran away from home, anything goes, I'm blamed. He doesn't want to know...he doesn't get involved.

These findings illustrate the particular situations in which many of the families were living, where they seemed to have problems with their children with little support to deal with them apart from what was on offer from the child care services. In many respects, this increased their dependency on the child protection service to be sensitive to, and meet, their requirements.

The fit between the needs expressed by the parents, and the service offered to them was good in some cases and some parents talked about the benefits of having 'somebody who is on your side' and 'getting somebody else's idea', getting a 'breather' (when a challenging teenager spent a short period in voluntary care) and resulting improvements in relationships between parents and children. Practical support and material help when given, was always valued and sometimes prioritised by parents. In some cases, it took a while for the benefits of certain interventions to be appreciated. The mother who had been advised to go to a women's refuge explained that she had gone along with the plan with considerable initial reluctance:

> When I first came to the refuge, I hated the place. I looked at [the social worker] and he said 'You will be here for three months' and I said 'You have to be out of your mind, I am not staying here for three months, I want to get out of this...'

But she also described how beneficial it had been for her:

...and I began to really like the place... I mean the laughs we used to have, me and the women down there... Yes, for my own safety and my child's safety, I think it was the best thing I ever...like I said to [the social worker], I could thank him... It was the best thing...it got me to look at myself and say look...the drinking isn't getting you anywhere...cop on to yourself...you are 30...you are not a spring chicken anymore, time to get something up here... So I am glad in a way I went up there, because I picked up a lot of things, it opened my eyes... Did you ever have anyone say to you, a good fright is the best thing for you? Like if you were in a car and you almost crashed into a bus...you'd say 'I'll always wear my seat belt'.

However, meeting the perceived needs of some other parents was not as feasible. A lone mother whose eldest child had severe behavioural difficulties had been offered first, a family support worker, and second, a child care worker to help her. Her contact with the statutory services had been initiated in the midst of inter-agency disagreement between a voluntary treatment service and the Health Board child protection service about whose responsibility it was to provide services for her, as well as the most appropriate type of intervention. No social worker had been allocated to her from the Health Board and communication between the agencies was very poor. The mother was unaware of the inter-agency difficulties, but was frustrated by what she considered were inappropriate services that were overwhelming her; first, the family support worker:

I felt I was being bombarded...they were all coming at me... I thought there was too many people to cope with and not enough time to fit in, if you understand... Being under a lot of pressure I couldn't even say what I was thinking, if you understand...

I didn't need somebody to come in and clean for me... I'm not...and in helping with [her son] I don't think anybody that I've got would have been cut out for it, they were the wrong person.

She was not impressed with the allocation of a child care worker either:

The first time we met her we went to the park, but like she said to me that I had great patience, she was losing hers...you know... And I said 'How does it feel for me then if she's losing her patience after such a short time?' You know...

When I interviewed her, the mother was well able to express what she wanted, but clearly had little confidence in what was being offered to her:

> I'd like a bit of advice, I don't mind people giving me support, like the psychologist was great, but then I felt too many people got involved in the whole thing... I could never really see anybody giving me the proper support and advice that I needed...like they were bringing these people in and I felt, oh God, these are not the people...for [her son], [it would need to be] somebody like...who has children of their own that would understand the situation a little bit better, you know.

The case where a three-year-old had been sexually abused by an adult neighbour had been closed after the child protection conference. This situation reflects the tendency highlighted by Thoburn *et al.* (1995) for less involvement of families in the child protection process if the alleged abuser was not a parent. The mother in this case was aware that the Health Board considered her child to be protected adequately, because the alleged abuse had been extra-familial, and the parents had shown appropriate concern. However, when I interviewed her, she was angry that the Health Board social worker had paid no heed to the very real needs they had as a family at that time:

> Ourselves...to a certain extent we felt that we were left high and dry and got no support and no proper advice on the way we should have handled it, and even more importantly, what has happened then to the abuser? That was another thing that was left completely...

> Nobody said 'We'll organise therapy for your daughter, and here is the name of somebody and here is how it can be done...' and whatever... I don't know, surely there is provision for such therapy to be organised... Or 'The parents themselves might need some counselling in the way they are going to handle it...' In fact, it was the view of [the assessment service] that maybe we needed some form of help or whatever... Again nothing was done, so I would question the [communication]... between [the assessment service] and the Health Board and their liaison with the Gardaí...We had absolutely nothing. We had ourselves to organise therapy for our daughter... I mean the whole thing...actually took an awful lot of our time and our money to organise... Not only is this a very traumatic event, but added to the trauma was the difficulty of dealing with people who weren't handling it properly.

Likewise, the mother who was cleared of physical abuse and neglect felt she was left 'high and dry' after the trauma of her interview with the social worker. Even though the social worker had assured her that no further action was necessary, she was deeply upset:

> They didn't help me at all. They questioned me, they told me the allegations, they blew me away with their letter, and…they gave me the allegations right there… I had my two kids with me… I'm dying inside… It was 'good-bye, thank you very much, you're exonerated…everything is fine…good-bye'.

> And when they exonerate you totally…to make you feel like you are not a bad person… I didn't feel like a good person coming out of that… [the social worker] was very tactful, and he was very understanding…but he obviously doesn't have the time to sit there and say 'You're not a bad person' and I just felt as low, as I possibly could feel… It was just a really bad time, and it was awful, because if there were times when if my son was bold after that, I would kneel down under the window sill and give out to him…shake my finger at him…I was terrified…who was watching me… That was what it left me with.

Women interviewed in Hooper's (1992) study sometimes felt that the implications for them of the discovery and investigation of their children's sexual abuse was unappreciated. This theory is reflected in Mrs M's account of her experience, which seemed to her to have been at odds with the expectations of her first social worker:

> [The social worker] knew that I hadn't understood because she said to me at one stage, unless I talked to her in confidence about how I feel and how everything is, I'll never get any further than I am. I'll just stay the way I am… That meant nothing to me only that I will never talk to her. And I turned around and said 'I'll never talk to you and I'll never tell you how I feel because I don't feel happy or comfortable', and that was the end of that. I don't think that should have been the end of that. Now, I think she should have realised that I didn't grasp the seriousness of it… I'm sure they have to accept that people don't understand everything in a case like this.

> I'm not saying it was [the social worker's] or anyone's fault… I just feel that they could make you… I'm sure that they knew that I didn't fully understand, I mean I was in shock, and I'd say I was in shock up to about December or January… And it was only then it was starting to hit

me…things were starting to come to me and I was saying 'ah sure'… I honestly believed…that by May we would be back together as a happy family as if nothing had happened. Now I can't believe that I believed that, how can anyone be so stupid, but then everyone here had believed it….We all believed it.

I don't know about other people, but I obviously didn't deal with it very well, I was in total shock, and disbelief. I just couldn't grasp all this, I really couldn't and it took me a long time, but I tell you, I paid dearly for it… I mean I paid by losing the children…

Conclusion

In examining the different perceptions of the parents as to how well their needs were understood and met, it appears that different variables interact to produce particular views. It was clear that the parents who felt their needs were being met were able to discern benefits for themselves and their children from their involvement with the child protection system. This was sometimes linked to the fact that they had initiated the first contact themselves, but not sufficiently often to claim this as a viable connection. Other influences reflected the degree of participation and involvement they experienced, the relationships they had with their workers, the 'user friendliness' or otherwise of the service, and the degree of 'fairness' they experienced. With the benefit of hindsight and knowledge of other aspects of the child protection process, it was possible in several instances to track themes that had emerged at earlier stages in these cases. For example, it could be seen that inter-professional and inter-agency tensions interfered with the child protection process to the extent that needs were ignored or met with inappropriate responses, and tasks 'fell between two stools'.

The other issue that stood out was one which recurs throughout the previous chapters: once 'child abuse' in its most manifest and visible forms was eliminated from the equation, the family ceased to concern the child protection services, even though it was, in some cases, left with serious problems which were likely to impact on the children's welfare. Examples of this were where a mother had been cleared of physical abuse and neglect and had subsequently suffered a recurrence of depression, and where a

child had been sexually abused by a neighbour but was deemed to be protected once her parents were aware of it. The data gathered in this phase of
the study challenge the notion that parents are, or can be treated as,
'passive agents' (Howe, 1992) and that they will uncompromisingly
co-operate with the child protection system and have their needs met by it.
While a number of parents indicated their satisfaction with the level of
service and the quality of relationships they had with their social workers,
there were many examples of poor communication, insensitivity and lack
of symmetry between the expressed needs of the parents and the response
of the system.

However, in many respects it is not possible to reach conclusions about
the experiences of parents without more complete reference to the case
data presented in the earlier chapters of this book. The next chapter will
attempt a fuller and concluding integration of these.

Chapter Seven

Concluding Analysis

A concern at the heart of this book has been the way in which an approach to child protection, termed by Parton *et al.* (1997) as the 'orthodox' or 'authoritative' version, is in danger of dominating the official discourse. Translating what is by its nature an uncertain and untidy activity, fraught with complexities, into a set of behaviours suggestive of rationality and passive adherence to regulation, is to give a very flawed impression of the 'real-life' work of child protection practitioners. In the process, the less visible processes and balancing strategies through which practitioners make sense of their work are being consistently occluded and are therefore unacknowledged. This study, by exposing the range and impact of those activities, has illustrated the dynamic nature of the child protection task. This concluding chapter now reflects on the research process, and the analysis of findings. Finally, it offers what I believe to be an informed perspective that goes beyond the 'official' rhetoric.

The child protection discourse

In this final chapter, it is important to clarify what precisely I mean by the 'official' and 'unofficial' discourses of child protection, and to contextualise them correctly. The child protection discourse that had developed in the UK by the 1990s is explained by Parton (1991, p.3) as a structure of 'historical and political frameworks of social organisation that make some social actions possible whilst precluding others'. Parton traces its evolution over the 1970s and 1980s through various social and political influences, partially constructed in response to the findings of empirical research, but seriously constrained by the decline in welfarism and the influence of child abuse inquiries, resulting in what he describes as a climate obsessed with concerns about risk, its assessment, monitoring and management. The development of child protection in Ireland has not been untouched by influences from other jurisdictions, but has unfolded in its own unique way, ultimately reflecting what Ferguson (1996, p.30) describes as 'the de-traditionalisation and liberalisation of Irish society'.

Historically, as Chapter One of this book has demonstrated, the response to child welfare concerns in Ireland, as in other countries, has acted at different times as a mechanism through which wider societal anxiety about deviance and delinquency, and aspirations towards moral reformism were realised. The development of services has tended, however, to be piecemeal and politically driven. The genesis of the current discourse lies in a number of developments, starting in the late sixties, which began to reflect a growing critique of services for children and of the legislative framework within which they operated. The *Report of the Kilkenny Incest Investigation* (Department of Health 1993) had an impact in Ireland comparable to that which followed the Colwell Inquiry in the UK, and brought about a 'radicalisation' of the child protection system (Ferguson 1996). Like the child abuse inquiries in Britain, the political and public reaction to the Kilkenny case precipitated not only a further consol-idation of awareness about child abuse (child sexual abuse in particular) but scrutiny of the services which were set up to address it.

Parton (1991, 1996b) and Howe (1992, 1996) describe the growth of the managerial component in child protection, where the skilled and in-depth elements of the work have given way to a practice governed by procedures and 'audit'. As Parton (1996b) contends, such approaches fail to acknowledge the central and pervasive concerns related to uncertainty and ambiguity. Howe (1996) believes that the increase in technicality has resulted in a diminution of practitioners' power and control over the way they use their skills. The same claims could not, I suggest, be made in relation to child protection work in Ireland, at least not yet. The backdrop of constitutional and ideological reverence for the family has made it less politically possible to acknowledge and own responsibility for a social problem such as child abuse, let alone set up complex administrative and managerial systems to address it. Commitment to policy development has tended to be less reflexive and more inert than, for example, in the UK. Yet the framework for the social organisation of child protection work is developing rapidly, heavily influenced by public and political opinion. This has been evidenced in what Howitt (1992) would describe as 'bureaucratic principles' underpinning, for example, the recommendations of the Kilkenny Report (Department of Health 1993) and other child abuse inquiries (Western Health Board 1996; North Western Health Board 1998) and new national child protection guidelines (Department of Health and Children 1999, Department of Health and Children 2002) Despite such increasing proceduralisation, however, there is little evidence from this study that practice was governed by even the level of bureaucracy that existed at the time. As I have shown, a number of political and cultural influences, reasoning processes and relational issues merge to 'construct' and make sense of the work in ways that bureaucratic principles cannot achieve.

Yet the purpose of this book has not been to undermine or deny the notion that social workers or other practitioners in child protection identify with or defer to agency function. Rather, it is to suggest that they actively weave their child protection roles instead of unquestioningly accepting the 'official' version. In the process, they create the 'unofficial' version. It was within such a critical context that this study set out to examine child protection practice, one of the principal aims being to contrast the 'real' work involved with the construction which is assumed in formal guidance and policy. By highlighting the ambiguities inherent in the day-to-day practice, the inadequacy of the official version as a yardstick against which practice may be either modelled or judged becomes visible.

Wise (1989), in her analysis of the epistemological basis from which the child protection discourse takes its identity, has named four assumptions which, she believes, underpin child abuse 'theory': that child abuse is predictable, clearly observable, and easily addressed, and that effective child protection work depends for its competence on inter-agency and inter-professional co-ordination. She proves her theory by examining these assumptions: first, in relation to a recent child abuse scandal and then comparing them with some examples from her own practice experience, the problematic and complex cases which are part and parcel of everyday child protection work. Not surprisingly, she found a lack of symmetry between the 'assumed' and the actual versions. In order to discuss and analyse the findings from this study, I have chosen a similar framework, which identifies six potentially false assumptions that I believe to underpin official policy and guidance on child protection and contrasts them with the reality that has emerged from this study of child protection practice.

The construction of child abuse

The first assumption upon which the technical/rational approach adopted in the official discourse of child protection rests is that child protection workers can, without demur, agree on a universal definition of child abuse and respond accordingly. As this book has demonstrated, acknowledging that a particular concern conforms to the notion of abuse or neglect is not simply a matter of having 'expert' knowledge or experience, or even checking a sign or symptom from a prescribed list. Dingwall *et al.* (1983, p.31) have proposed that 'abuse and neglect are the products of complex processes of identification, confirmation and disposal, rather than something which was inherent in a child's presenting condition'. In a similar vein, examination of the practice of local authority social workers has demonstrated that the act of designating a concern about a child or children into the category of 'child abuse' is heavily laden with presumptions and prospective obligations, and needs to be judged in that context. If, for example, a definition of 'abuse' is adopted, the corollary is that it should be investigated, with all that that entails. If, on the other hand, the notion of 'abuse' is discounted, social workers and families are exempted from that process.

At this point in the exploration of decision-making, the methodological approach merged very successfully with the objectives of the study in that it enabled a broad, contextualised, picture to emerge, in which were manifested the mundane as well as the unusual happenings. This became obvious when the nature of referrals to the child protection system was considered. Despite the 'popular' image of child abuse that is portrayed in checklists of signs and symptoms, the reported concerns upon which this study was based only occasionally conformed to what I have termed a 'text book' presentation. The 'text book' appellation derives from the popular notion of child abuse informed, as Thorpe (1994) asserts, by knowledge about 'worst possible cases' and constituted through 'diagnostic inflation' (Dingwall 1989, p.129). What this study found was that lack of clarity regarding the thresholds beyond which 'concerns' became 'abuse' inevitably led to the adoption of some rationalising techniques, which drew on an amalgam of professional experience and personal values, derived from the ideological perspectives of practitioners. These were manifested through the high level of pre-screening which was applied to reports before they entered the formal child abuse system; a process that appeared to be determined by three motives.

The first pre-screening device had two purposes, to keep the level of work manageable and at the same time, preserve a scale according to which a label of 'seriousness' could be assigned so as not to devalue the system. It was left to the workers themselves to apply a 'principle of specificity' (Thorpe 1994, p.5) to the 'child abuse' concerns that were reported to them. This was achieved, not by measuring the degree of actual harm, but through a process of interpreting *available* circumstantial information and ascribing a value to it. As Chapter Two has illustrated, the rationale applied could include a judgement of the character or reputation of the informant, which could lend to or detract from the likelihood of an ascription of 'seriousness' to the concern. Another means of preserving a threshold of seriousness was the (unacknowledged) norm whereby the social workers would not 'chase' further information about referrals, even from reputable informants, if the referrers themselves did provide enough detail to *compel* it. The social workers appeared to operate on the assumption that referrers would act responsibly, therefore if they failed to respond to a request to provide more substantial information, this acted to dilute the potential gravity of the matters they had reported in the first instance.

Anxiety about the potential impact on a family of an investigation constituted a second element in the pre-screening process, and was an issue to which practitioners accorded a high level of sensitivity. The crucial point beyond which speculation became realisation was pivotal to the outcome of this decision-making. It was most clearly at this juncture that Dingwall

et al.'s (1983) 'rule of optimism' was visible. Through this device, the practitioners voiced their unease with the imposition of standards, about
'slapping' children, for instance, or 'different social value systems' particularly when the reported incidents appeared to be the least adverse
elements in the lives of the families concerned. Dread of 'devastating' a
family by their intervention also appeared to orientate workers towards
the construction of whatever evidence was available in a positive light, and
made them disinclined to search for more information that could potentially discredit that view.

The third determinant of 'pre-screening' which became visible in the
study was the social workers' pessimism about the benefit or likely
effectiveness of intervention into what might be described as 'convoluted'
situations, for instance, those presenting with 'chronic' neglect and all its
associated conditions such as addiction, poverty, mental illness, and
general marginalisation. Examination of the responses given to concerns
of this type indicated a trend whereby, if the evidence of child neglect or
maltreatment were highly visible (e.g. if a child had been literally
abandoned), a 'strong' investigative response would be elicited. However
in many instances, either the evidence would not be judged sufficiently
'incriminating' to *compel* a response from families, or it was accepted that
the family would not have either the capacity or the necessary resources to
change. The root of the dilemma appeared to lie in the social workers'
sense that the forensic approach which is central to child protection
investigations had little to offer situations that were not amenable to either
'warnings' or accessible solutions.

A similar trend is apparent in the literature. Thorpe (1994, p.196) for
example, considering the 'overrepresentation of poor and disadvantaged
people' in child abuse statistics, argues that 'child protection' does little to
improve the lot of many children who come into its net, and in fact
performs poorly in relation to 'neglect' cases. The reason, he explains, is
because the 'technology' and 'knowledge base' that is constructed around
'child abuse' does not represent the majority of those who actually come
into contact with the system. Gibbons *et al.* (1995) similarly found that
'neglect' referrals were most likely to be filtered out of the system at an
early stage. This, they believe, is linked to the focus of assessment that

determines if children are 'in need of protection' rather than 'in need'. Stevenson (1996, p.13) explains the 'neglect of neglect' in the same terms, but also highlights the links between neglect and poverty, and the way that social workers have become used to certain families 'bumping along the bottom'. Perceiving the parents to be under intolerable strain practitioners, according to Stevenson, 'are reluctant to make the judgements which lead to the finding of neglect' (p.16). The social workers in this study were clearly operating within the same parameters, which they used as channels through which to divert families from the system.

The screening devices that have just been discussed operated to eliminate over half of the allegations prior to all but cursory investigation, by re-framing them in such a way that the 'danger' or 'risk' elements that had caused the original concern were minimised or excised. All of these decisions employed a high level of sense-making, not necessarily on individual levels but often by collegial consensus, albeit fragile, after long and tortuous debate that invoked different personal value systems, perspectives and experiences. In practice, the balance more often than not swung towards non-intervention when the pros and cons were weighed up against each other: the potential for effective change as against the uncertainty, upset and possible aggression which would be met if parents were confronted with an accusation of child maltreatment. The sense-making process itself appeared to be comprised of the aforementioned determinants, but was equally coloured by judgements about the character of referrers, and aspects of Dingwall et al.'s (1983) 'cultural relativism', whereby different norms are applied to different social and ethnic groups. For example, despite what is known about the disadvantages and hazards faced by Irish traveller families (O'Higgins 1993; Task Force on the Travelling Community 1995), the findings of this research have shown how a significant diversity of standards was apparent in the responses to reports about them. Although the presence of minority ethnic groups in the study was small, there was evidence to indicate, for example, that living conditions that would have been considered unacceptable within the settled or indigenous community were tolerated in relation to particular groups. This is of particular significance given the growing diversity of Irish society and the need to develop culturally sensitive methods of working with refugees and asylum seekers (Torode, Walsh and Woods 2001).

As I have already indicated, the measurement of 'good enough' care was, in a paradoxical fashion, inversely associated with the parents' anticipated capacity to change it, so that certain, particularly marginalised, social groups were allowed a great deal of latitude before the 'rule of optimism' (Dingwall *et al.* 1983) was breached. In fact, little attempt was made to grapple with the dilemmas presented by cultural or social differences and as has been demonstrated, the social workers' method of resolving the issue was more often than not achieved by distancing themselves, either discounting the concern or devolving the responsibility for dealing with it to some other agency.

Assessment criteria

A second assumption inherent in the official version of child protection is that the system, within its present social and organisational context, has the capacity to make definitive judgements in relation to the concerns about children that are reported to it. This notion resembles one of the 'elements in common-sense accounting for child abuse work' that Wise (1989, p.503) has identified, that child abuse is 'obvious' and that once identified, renders itself open to the competent application of a clear solution. While Wise drew attention to the invisibility, for example, of emotional abuse, which is often a cumulative condition, this book is concerned less with the *nature* of the harm itself, than with the *limits of assessment* within the framework the practitioners used. The unique advantages of the qualitative methodological approach to the research permitted, at this point, an exploration of what Denzin and Lincoln (1994, pp.5–6) term the 'actor's perspective' through 'rich descriptions' and managed to get a sense of the criteria which determined the levels of seriousness accorded to the different concerns.

The workers were well aware that, within the 'liberal compromise' (Dingwall *et al.* 1983), unless there was fairly tangible evidence to suggest serious injury or harm, there was only so far that they could pursue investigations. This study has shown that within this sensitive context, risk or danger in a situation is frequently endorsed or mitigated by measuring the response of parents to the experience of being investigated. As the research findings have indicated, favourable assessments would often be complemented by some degree of positive evidence of parenting skill, in the form of 'well cared for' appearances of the children involved or a 'snapshot' of an acceptable quality of relationship between parents and children. By association, the excuse of 'natural love', a constituent element of the 'rule of optimism' which acts as a 'powerful part of the operational framing of front-line work' (Dingwall *et al.* 1983, p.87), appeared to exonerate parents who were able to demonstrate to the investigating workers their capacity, in keeping with their 'humanity', to love their children.

Analysis of the various rationales employed to mitigate certain acts or omissions in relation to children highlights the important role of 'contrition'. If parents could indicate, by their attitude to the worker, that a warning had been heard and accorded due gravity, a sort of mutual bargaining process was negotiated, and even if the concern had been substantiated, it was unlikely that further child protection interventions would ensue. If, on the other hand, parental compliance did not materialise or was withdrawn, 'parental incorrigibility' (Dingwall *et al.* 1983) was established, and the 'rule of optimism' was breached. This process also replicates Thorpe's (1994, p.73) conclusion that the capacity of caregivers to co-operate with child protection workers, particularly in relation to 'neglect' concerns, represented a particular example of situated moral reasoning which gained extra merit when inter-linked with other signs of good moral character.

What also emerged from the data was not so much a confidence placed by the workers in this type reasoning behaviour, but a sense of resignation on their part that it was simply not feasible in certain instances to 'know' what had happened. For instance, without witnesses it was nearly impossible for practitioners to know whether or not something *really* had occurred. This was at times coupled with a confusion as to which of the many adverse factors in the children's lives the assessment should be focused on. In situations where the evidence was, as one worker described it, 'nebulous' they were reluctant to be 'abrasive' in their approach and so they accepted its limitations, acting, though not consciously, within the 'liberal compromise'. The belief that, much of the time, they had 'nothing to offer' beyond following 'the letter of the law' appeared to endorse their reluctance to pursue more intrusive measures and allow a degree of ambivalence to permeate their assessment criteria. Of the 28 child abuse allegations that were investigated by the statutory social workers by means of a personal interview with the parents or carers of the children, 14 were kept open for further work. The other 14 were closed, with no further action taken during the fieldwork period. Three of the child abuse investigations devolved to non-statutory agencies were kept open for further work, in one case by a social worker in a clinic for children with disabilities, and in two others by treatment agencies. As the study has demonstrated, no explicit criteria operated to ensure that all the agencies operated similar child protection practices.

The myth of 'inter-agency co-operation'

The national child abuse guidelines (Department of Health 1987) which were in operation at the time the fieldwork for this study was conducted and the later published guidelines for the *Notification of Child Abuse Cases between Health Boards and the Gardaí* (Department of Health 1995), both comment on the importance of a multi-disciplinary, co-ordinated approach to child protection work. It is reiterated in the more recently published national child protection and welfare guidelines (Department of Health and Children 1999). The notion that a co-ordinated approach necessarily makes for a better practice is unquestioningly presumed in these documents. This is despite evidence that not only do different disciplines bring different ethical and normative value systems to bear on their decision-making strategies, but that the inevitable fragmentation of work can often serve to minimise its effectiveness (Dingwall *et al.* 1983; Hallett and Birchall 1992; Reder *et al.* 1993; Hallett 1995; Scott 1997).

This study has challenged the validity of the assumption that, first, such unity is possible, and second, that given the acknowledged difficulties, the achievement of inter-agency and inter-professional co-ordination is a useful aspiration. Several theories drawn from the literature can be used to explain the fragile base upon which assumptions about co-operation are founded. Whittington (1983, pp.270–271), commenting on accountability within the 'welfare network', asserts that in the absence of joint rules, divisions of labour or an overall authority, agreement on courses of action have to be 'negotiated' involving a process of 'give and take, politicking, diplomacy, bargaining and argument' (p.272) within the limits set by organisational factors. This study has highlighted the way that negotiations around the sensitive area of child abuse were extremely fraught and, for the reasons outlined by Whittington, tended to be inconclusive, sometimes resulting in an impasse regarding the ownership of certain roles and obligations. In addition, there is the nature of the work itself which, Blyth and Milner (1990, p.197) argue, militates against effective inter-agency co-operation. They refer to Hughes' (1958, p.49) appellation of 'dirty work' as 'those activities which have to be done but are nevertheless distasteful in the doing' and identify its applicability to child protection activity. Cultural norms also operate to enforce this notion. Butler (1996, p.312) argues that 'child protection work in Ireland has the potential to become even "dirtier" than it is in Britain', linked as it is to the ambivalence which exists about state intrusion into the family, and the greater possibility of 'opprobrium' attaching to practitioners whose duties involve 'policing' elements. The reluctance of non social work professionals to take on this mantle emanates, according to Butler, from 'clashes of professional culture' (p.310) and results in the burdening of social workers with the 'unenviable task' of carrying out the social control functions of child protection activity.

An important constituent factor in decision-making about the investigation of reports, and one which crops up at various points along the careers of cases, is the notion of responsibility. As Hallett and Birchall (1992) point out, power forms a significant element of an occupation's self-image and status, and can reside in legal responsibilities, authority and command of resources. Potential for tense relationships between social workers and other professionals lies in the conflict between, on the one hand, the statutory social workers' responsibility and on the other, their lack of authority over those professionals on whose co-operation they depend. There was strong evidence in this study not only of struggles related to power and responsibility, but also of their impact on the processing of referrals. Conflict appeared, to an extent, to be connected with professional identity. Certain practitioners were not inclined to integrate a sense of obligation or responsibility or even awareness of child abuse issues in their overall professional task. Nor did they believe that their own ethical norms or standards were congruent with those of the statutory agencies. Crucially, however, the link between *assertion* of role boundaries and *avoidance* of the policing, or nastier elements of child protection work became increasingly visible. As a consequence, and in the absence of any administrative mandate to share or divide work in any particular fashion, inter-agency and inter-professional hostilities frequently dominated the professional response to child care concerns. Even failures of communication and organisational weaknesses that appeared to undermine co-operation seemed at times to be linked with unacknowledged battles over the ownership of responsibility. These behaviours appeared to provoke other professionals and agencies into defensive positions, expending a lot of energy into 'turf wars' at the expense of good practice.

Findings from this study indicate the existence of a range of impediments to useful, joint work between different professions and agencies. Some factors were associated with professionals in specific occupations, who did not either identify with or accommodate child protection work in their overall occupational tasks. On occasions, this separation stemmed from sheer lack of information. For example, the majority of general practitioners involved in the study were unfamiliar with the child protection system, having neither contact with the Health Board or knowledge of the national child abuse procedures. Other obstacles to co-operation were more philosophical in origin, emanating from different and conflicting value perspectives. The implications of these sometimes deeply entrenched, inter-professional disagreements for the children and families caught up in the system were quite serious. Certain locations, such as conferences, were frequently dominated by unacknowledged tensions which bore little relevance to the welfare or protection of the children concerned. These findings replicate the identification in the literature of negative dynamics, such as the 'hidden agendas' and stereotyping observed by Hallett and Stevenson (1980). As Reder *et al.* (1993, p.67) point out, case conferences are vulnerable to the same group processes as any other meeting, 'attendances and absences, chairing, alliances, hierarchy and projection' all influencing the final decision. There was evidence in the research to uphold this theory, including examples of 'dormant professional rivalries' and 'exaggerated hierarchies', and several instances where it was clear that pre-set attitudes and beliefs were carried into the meetings by participants.

As case careers in this study moved forward, there was further evidence of Hallett's (1995) assertion that commitment to co-operation diminishes once the investigative stages of child protection work have passed. Reder *et al.*'s (1993) observation that the behaviour of professionals can come to mirror the splitting, chaos and other unhealthy dynamics in families was reflected in certain cases. Indeed, when viewed in terms of an interacting system, the professional network bore a strong resemblance to a dysfunctional family, with elements of competitiveness, scapegoating, insensitivity and rigidity.

Sadly, there was no evidence that any attempt to ameliorate this situation was being either taken or contemplated by any of the managers involved, and there was little sense that the deeper issues, which have been highlighted in this study, were either acknowledged or understood by them. An assumption that professionals in child protection can or will, in such a context of conflicted power and responsibility, work together to achieve a compromise on the 'division of regulatory labour' (Dingwall *et al.* 1983) appears quite naive.

If these findings are judged through a sociological perspective, such as the 'liberal compromise' conceived by Dingwall *et al.* (1983), it could be proposed that the relatively low rate of investigation and intervention is less reflective of the practice of individual workers, or even of the team culture, than it is of a general societal attitude to the version of child protection officially promulgated. A cultural ideology that upholds the rights of families to autonomy, combined with a lack of professional trust or even interest in the statutory child protection system, is indicative of a society that has not fully worked out an acceptable relationship between families and the state. Statutory social workers in child protection, it appears, are left to interpret the boundaries of this relationship, mediating between their professional values and the administrative requirements of their agency function. At a micro-level, social workers find themselves suffering from a type of cognitive dissonance and, as Powell (1997) observes, are often deeply demoralised by this conflict.

The 'jokers in the pack'

So far, this analysis of the research findings has exposed the work in child protection as a process replete with interacting elements which challenge the more or less static nature of the officially assumed relationship between the child protection discourse and the practitioners whose job it is to operationalise it. The fourth assumption that is disputed by this research concerns itself with another dynamic component of the child protection system, referred to by Howe (1992, p.506) as the 'jokers in the pack': the parents at whom most of the work is directed. The assumption to which I refer is that parents will accommodate the child protection discourse to the extent of accepting the version or measure of 'adequate' parenting that is presented to them, and willingly conform to the required standard. There is also a presumption that it is the social worker, not the parent, who decides at what point this aspiration has been realised. This assumption has been challenged here on a number of different levels, and areas have been identified where little or no meeting of minds between practitioners and parents occurs. The study has shown, for example, the different sense-making strategies employed by both parties with regard to parenting standards, in terms of what is 'good enough', and where personal values and professional duties frequently conflicted. Hooper (1992, p.162) has criticised statutory social workers for having the sort of expectations of mothers, which they clearly fail to meet themselves, in terms of 'doing enough' for children in a context of contradictory societal expectations and limited resources. This study has demonstrated too that social workers permitted themselves a degree of risk taking which they were not prepared to allow parents to exercise.

Reder *et al.* (1993), viewing child abuse cases through a systemic framework, illustrated the level of power exercised by parents in their efforts to keep social workers at a distance. Similarly, Parton *et al.* (1997) used social work records to illustrate the degree to which relationships between practitioners and parents were *negotiated*, implying the utilisation of control on each side. The literature also identifies situations where the power balance is less in the parents' favour. Cleaver and Freeman (1995) observe that the more convergence there is between the 'operational perspectives' of practitioners and parents, the more favourable the outcome of work is likely to be. Examples from this research confirm their theory, indicating that while good relationships could be forged in the context of child protection interventions, this was more likely to happen when levels of agreement about the child care concern and about the culpability for it were high.

This research has shown, through the cases studied, the level to which parents were able to determine the frequency of their contact with the child protection system and ultimately the termination of that intervention. Yet there was little evidence of practitioners capitalising on the capacity of clients to shape their own destinies to any great extent. In fact, the notion of 'partnership' with parents was best encapsulated in the aspiration of most practitioners to reach a stage where parents could participate fully at case conferences. Yet although studies in the UK Department of Health research programme (Thoburn *et al.* 1995; Farmer and Owen 1995) confirm the benefits of sensitively anticipated parental participation, strong reservations remain. Bell (2000) cautions that while parents prefer to be at conferences, the degree to which partnership and empowerment are possible is limited. Dingwall, Eekelaar and Murray (1995) in a postscript to their earlier (1983) study claim that parental inclusion at case conferences is not the panacea that was anticipated. They suggest that in practice, the 'new-style case conferences' operating in the UK may simply reproduce many of the procedural defects in the traditional style of proceedings, 'with parents being confronted with the professionals' case against them and asked to accept this without serious forensic test' (p.253). If a parent does not agree to plans predefined by professionals, they suggest, this is likely to be interpreted as further evidence of their 'incorrigibility', legitimating compulsory action. Likewise, Corby *et al.* (1996), sense a 'misplaced optimism' in the popular notion of parental involvement, suggesting that parental participation is more likely to be related to the 'compliance' rather than the 'openness' of parents. Corby *et al.*'s central argument is that the denial of the power differentials undermines the usefulness of involving parents at all.

The debate is likely to go on, but in the meantime there was little evidence in this study that the essential issues had been grasped, or that either the rights or the ability of parents to shape the nature of interventions, was fully acknowledged. Ironically, although the statutory social workers were prepared, within the 'liberal compromise' to display a high degree of deference towards family autonomy *prior* to intervening, once the threshold of entering the system had been passed, they appeared disinclined to capitalise on families' natural resourcefulness to the same extent.

The gendered nature of child protection practice

In its challenge to the static nature of the child protection system assumed in the official discourse, this book has indicated the level and number of unacknowledged processes that constantly interact and exert their influence to produce a type of practice that is far from the orthodoxy expected. It has also drawn attention to another important feature of the child protection discourse, one which has begun to attract a lot of attention over the past decade, through its association with the feminist interest in child abuse and family violence, and that is its gender blindness. The fifth assumption underpinning the child protection discourse that has been disputed by this research is its 'neutrality'. The findings of other studies in relation to the over-representation of mothers in the child protection system have been replicated here. Although not all initial 'child abuse' referrals were made with sufficient detail to make an accurate demographic analysis, it did appear that lone parent families, almost all headed by mothers, dominated the statistics, following the trend noted in studies by Thorpe (1994) Farmer and Owen (1995) and Gibbons, Conroy and Bell (1995). More than half of the cases that were subject to case conferences and allocated for further work were comprised of female lone parent families. Research in Ireland (McCashin 1996) indicates that lone parents as a category have lower incomes by the standards of Irish society at large. In the same vein, Thorpe (1994) has analysed the type of difficulties that affect women caring for children on their own and the professional responses that tend to focus almost exclusively on how they fulfil their parental roles, rather than on their personal and social problems. Yet though several of the single mothers interviewed for this research did appear to experience a level of shared understanding between themselves and the social workers, there was little evidence of any special consideration of lone motherhood and its associated stresses in the professional discourse.

This book has shown that in terms of practice, the focus of child protection attention and adjudication was unapologetically on mothers even when fathers were known to be responsible for the alleged concern or harm, reflecting two important issues. One is that mothers are, even when they have male partners, clearly allocated the responsibility for the care and protection of their children. The second issue also has serious practice implications, and concerns the way that the system deals with men's violence. When responses were considered through this perspective, there appeared a pattern of practitioner avoidance and mitigation of men where aggression might be anticipated. The tendency for such gendered practice to conceal itself in the way that responsibility and culpability is framed within the child protection discourse has been noted in the literature (Gordon 1989; Milner 1993; Daniel and Taylor 2001). This study has demonstrated the way in which it is compounded by practitioners who act both within societal and cultural expectations, but also out of self-protection, in an occupational framework that has not come to grips with unsafe aspects of the job.

The gendered paradigm operated by the child protection system was illustrated in particular by the M case. The participatory nature of the qualitative research approach allowed the unfolding of the 'story' to become visible through different perspectives, illustrating the unique range of experiences to which families where child sexual abuse has occurred are subject. The first gender issue was the nature of the abuse committed by the father against the weaker and more vulnerable family members. The mother's painful journey through the 'discovery' process illustrated another issue which was not particularly understood or responded to by the child protection system, but which could be analysed through Hooper's (1992) stages of: 'suspecting', 'not knowing' and 'knowing'. The study illustrated a further complex dimension to this type of situation, that even when efforts are made to appreciate the mother's victimisation, the children can still remain vulnerable (Wise 1995), resulting almost inevitably in conflict between mothers and social workers. Yet the research has also offered a different case example of where the application of a feminist approach which consistently defines women as 'victims' rather than 'villains' to cases of child abuse appeared to be highly problematic, in keeping with Featherstone's (1996) reservations about its 'universalist' applicability. What one father described as 'the motherhood' syndrome apparently mitigated, as far as the child protection system was concerned, any complaints that he reported regarding his wife's care of the children. His social worker agreed that he had become a 'victim of feminism', illustrating the way in which practice paradigms born out of aspirations to support the oppressed can paradoxically compound prejudice and discrimination. As Featherstone (1997, pp.428–429) asserts, any theory must be 'wary of fixed notions' concerning men, women and children, and fuller understandings of gender as well as questions of power, need to be explored.

The child in child protection

The sixth assumption upon which the official version of child protection is founded concerns the child centredness of, or even the presence of children in, the child protection discourse. Reading through the research findings, it is difficult to get a picture of the children to whose safety and welfare the reports referred, and with whose protection the system is allegedly concerned. Neither their views nor their contributions are represented; nor is the extent to which they shaped the outcomes of investigation or intervention. Parton *et al.* (1997, p.96) argue that:

> Child protection depends a great deal on the social construction of children and the ways in which children subject to child protection intervention are seen as cultural products and become objects of organisational interest.

The point here is that 'children' in child protection are configured in terms of those aspects of their safety and welfare that are of interest to the discourse that has been set up around the problem of 'child abuse'.

The 'absence' of children in this book reflects two important issues. The first one concerns the methodological paradigm adopted by the study.

Reflecting on Trinder's (1996) assertion that methodologies are not 'innocent' I need, at this point, to acknowledge the failure of this study to reflect the perspectives of children, both by their exclusion from the research process itself, and in terms of the approach taken. Guba and Lincoln (1994, p.115) stress that the 'inquirer' should, in qualitative research, facilitate a 'multivoiced' reconstruction by *all* participants of his or her own construction. Otherwise, they suggest, the inquirer's voice is that of the 'disinterested scientist' who simply acts to 'justify actions, policies and change proposals'. Hill (1997, p.171) too reiterates an obvious but crucial point: the importance of the child's voice in relation to services that have as their aim the furtherance of children's welfare. He joins in critiques of the earlier tendencies within sociology to treat children as 'objects of socialisation', rarely engaging them as subjects. It has to be said that this study has been equally guilty in that regard. At the outset, I stated that my position in this study had to acknowledge my 'history' as a practitioner at the time the fieldwork was carried out, and it now appears that an element of the reality which I brought to the research was the tendency to interpret children's voices through a parental construction.

Yet this failure cannot be separated from the second issue, which has to do with the way that child abuse and child protection are organisationally defined, a point which will be developed below. In some respects, the dearth of children's perspectives in the research illustrates the way in which my approach allowed itself to be led by the child protection discourse, where, it would appear, children are largely 'silent'. I have shown that only in a minority of instances have investigating social workers actually laid their eyes on the children who were the subjects of reported concerns, and in many of the situations where children were seen, it seemed almost by chance that they happened to be available. At case conferences, apart from the contributions of teachers, public health nurses, some general practitioners and professionals in child psychiatry, analysis of the discussion indicated that the main focus was not on the present 'state' of the children, but on the actual incident which had provoked the child protection concern, the culpability more often than not of the mother, and her capacity to heed the 'warnings' given to her. The way in which the often hostile inter-professional dynamics at such meetings dominated the decision-making processes and outcomes has also illustrated the lack of child-centredness in such settings.

It would not be correct to claim that practitioners ignored the children in the course of longer term work; there was evidence in several cases that the children were singled out for individual attention and ongoing work. Ultimately however, as the last two chapters have shown, the quality of the relationship between the social workers and the parents, usually mothers, determined the nature and timing of the work. Association thus defined the protection and welfare of the children. National guidelines and procedures emphasise the need to encourage the participation of children in plans that concern them (Department of Health [UK] 1999; Department of Health and Children [Ireland] 1999) Yet the absence of children in the discourse is inextricably linked to the elements which combine to construct it; the 'liberal compromise' (Dingwall *et al.* 1983), the gendered nature of the work (Milner 1993), and the interactional processes operating in the system as a whole (Reder *et al.* 1993). Similarly, there is evidence that children have, to an extent, been sequestered by the tendency of the child protection system to define their protection and welfare in terms of future risk and past incidences rather than their current emotional and psychological well-being (Thorpe 1994; Gibbons *et al.* 1995; Farmer and Owen 1995).

The 'organisational' version of child protection

Finally, and not unconnected with the last point, one specific and unacknowledged function of the child protection discourse has been its propensity to redefine child abuse *organisationally.* At the outset of this book, I pointed out that of the 237 referrals to the social work service in the area under study, 165 were designated into categories other than 'child abuse/neglect'. Only ten of these referrals received any follow up, compared with the 72 reports categorised as 'child abuse/neglect', most of which were subjected to at least a cursory enquiry. It was not within the remit of this study to analyse the non-child abuse/neglect reports, but the categories to which they were allocated suggest that some level of adversity was being experienced by the adults and children concerned.

Statutory social work, as I have demonstrated, and as others have pointed out (Ferguson 1996; Eastern Health Board 1997; Buckley *et al.* 1997; Ferguson and O'Reilly 2000), has become dominated by child protection. This study has illustrated the extent to which client 'need' is now interpreted according to whether or not it fits into agency function. Analysis of the 'filtering' criteria employed offered examples of the elimination without investigation of problems of domestic violence, inadequate housing, and personal stress. Even within the work considered eligible for attention, unless the 'child abuse' so defined conformed to a designated norm, it was discounted. Chapter Three has demonstrated how the cases which were recommended for further action were those where the 'harm' was highly visible and were endorsed by the involvement and interest of professionals outside the statutory system. A high proportion of 'neglect' reports were eliminated, even prior to the investigation stage, and no case of alleged emotional abuse was followed up with an investigation. Howe (1992, p.497) argues that the emerging discourse with its 'administrative and judicial attitude' excludes the rehabilitation of 'poorly performing families' by the substitution of child protection in a narrow sense. This trend has also been noted in Australia, where Thorpe (1994, p.192) found that interventions in 'neglect' or 'at risk' cases were not focused 'in a genuine sense' on resolving the problems of families marginalised by poverty and/or addiction problems. Rather, he suggests, 'the social welfare discourse responds with a particular type of short term (punitive) remedy', and is more suited to the 'straightforward "rescue" interventions required of victims of assault'. The UK child protection research overview (Department of Health [UK] 1995) confirms that the long-term damage to children caused by neglect and emotional abuse is no less serious than physical or sexual abuse, yet is inadequately accommodated by the child protection framework as it is currently operated. This book has also illustrated how the separation of 'child abuse' from other concerns has also served to allow certain professions to divorce themselves from aspects of the work, and devolve responsibility for them to the statutory services, particularly social workers.

Ironically, when the evidential or 'juridical lens' (Parton 1991) is applied to the child protection work featuring in this research, it can be seen that the number of legal interventions actually taken was negligible. Civil actions to remove or keep children from their parents' care were taken in only two cases. In the cases where crimes were judged to have been committed, no prosecutions ensued either because the evidence was considered inadequate or because the family declined to press charges. As Wattam (1997, p.105) argues, the notion of 'protection through prosecution', which is neither achieved nor achievable in the vast majority of cases, is highly fallible, and has serious costs in terms of the traumatic impact on complainants, particularly child witnesses. Yet as she points out, notions of the utility or desirability of legal interventions are rarely challenged. At the same time, as we have seen in Ireland, the criminalisation of child maltreatment is becoming integral to the child protection discourse since the implementation of the guidelines on *Notification of Suspected Cases of Child Abuse between the Gardaí and the Health Boards* (Department of Health 1995) and later, *Children First: National Guidelines for the Protection and Welfare of Children* (Department of Health and Children 1999).

Risk and child protection

The weaknesses in the child protection discourse need to be explained at a broader societal level. Parton (1996b), Howe (1996), Powell (1997) and Parton and O'Byrne (2000) have written about social work in a post-modern society, where individual responsibility and freedom have become paramount, and traditional certainties have been discredited. What Powell (1997, p.63) terms 'an environment defined by the calculation of risk' has, apparently, emerged. This development Parton (1996b) tells us, is a consequence of the social fragmentation brought about by the collapse of welfarism and the growth of neo-liberalism and its accompanying insecurities, which have provided a rationale for attempting to address and cope with the new situation. Trust now has to be underpinned by accountability and within this paradigm, the objective becomes the identification of 'dangerousness'. Judgements regarding 'concerns' about children are reached according to a normative framework that determines whether or not a particular type of risk is present. In the meantime, the definitions of child abuse have widened considerably, to the point where it is acknowledged that not all aspects of it are visible, or even measurable;

evidence or proof of its existence have begun to depend on 'expert' knowledge. Consequently, adjudications are made on a basis that not only relies extensively on a culturally defined version of adequate child care, but is itself prone to error.

Within this discourse, there is a strong concentration on the personal and moral qualities of individuals within a specific and limited environment, with very little reference to structural or broader social environments. In such a context, the child protection discourse is based on the notion that the work carries within it the potential for a high level of certainty, that risks are calculable, and that all the actors within the system are the passive recipients and conveyors of information and expertise that can effectively address a range of predictable and manageable circumstances. The study upon which this book is based has shown the weakness in such a premise. In keeping with the theoretical framework adopted, it has demonstrated the presence of a secondary or parallel framework for practice, which is constantly being negotiated and is maintained by the practitioners themselves as a way of dealing with what Pithouse (1987, p.5) describes as 'the dilemmas and unpalatable issues that permeate the occupational task'.

A central objective of this study has been to contribute to the knowledge base by explaining the complexities and contradictions inherent in child protection 'work'. In doing so it has also inevitably represented the phenomenon of what is known as 'child abuse' in terms of a range of possible ideologies and aspirations about how parents/carers should behave and how children should be cared for. The inseparability of these phenomena means that both the professional and political dimensions of the child protection discourse need to be addressed.

At a professional level, the findings from this research indicate that many of the tenets upon which social work was traditionally based have been subsumed by the official, organisational discourse that prevails in statutory agencies. As Stevenson (1997) has pointed out, bureaucratic structures may often run counter to available knowledge and theory, and stifle professional development. The exercise of 'good judgement' is, she argues, the critical foundation upon which child abuse policies and procedures depend. Good judgement, as Stevenson defines it, depends on the interaction between knowledge, skills and values, and is increasingly difficult to achieve in a context of pressures, complications and sensitivities. The child protection discourse should be driven by good professional judgements not vice versa, and in order to ensure that this happens, practitioners need to be constantly aware of what Stevenson terms 'societal value tensions'.

At a theoretical level, Ferguson (1997, p.232) argues for the adoption of 'a critical theory of child protection without guarantees'. By this, he essentially intends professionals and lay people to become 'reskilled' by confronting risk in a reflective and reflexive fashion which incorporates an understanding of the underlying social conditions which shape the work of child protection, at the same time acknowledging that failure in expert human systems is 'ineradicable'. Stevenson (1997, p.7) too recognises the need for agencies to give workers opportunities for reflective practice, and for social workers to overcome their reluctance to 'make explicit the place which knowledge/theory should have in professional activity', including what she describes as 'practice theory', for example, 'knowledge' about child development combined with 'theories' about attachment.

At a societal level, there has to be an acknowledgement that child protection cannot be categorised simply as success or failure. Howe (1992, p.497) argues that the bureaucratisation of social work which has followed the emergence of 'child abuse' has attempted to develop solutions 'within a single conceptual outlook' which sought to deal with the work of child protection in a systematic and uniform manner, thereby making social workers into 'passive agents'. The child protection discourse in Ireland, while not as bureaucratic as that which operates, for example, in the UK, is fundamentally concerned with risk management, and is becoming more so; the way in which the 'work' has been illustrated in this book bears testimony to this. A senior Health Board administrator (Doherty 1996) has identified the 'moral panic' which has followed disclosures and child abuse scandals in Ireland in recent years which, he observes, is:

> ...characterised by a desperate search for simple solutions based on unrealistic and often contradictory expectations, and a failure to grasp the realities of dealing with child protection situations. (p.103)

There must be a questioning of the notion that all social problems can be managed by professionals, and that child protection agencies can guarantee that parents will not harm their children. This questioning needs to transcend professional debates and enter the public and political consciousness in order, as Ferguson (1997) argues, to 'liberate' professionals so that they may 'mobilize' major social problems and reduce their impact.

The growth of a discourse that is essentially bureaucratic, defined by management and prescription without consideration of the imperfections, organic weaknesses or uncertainties of 'real' life, only serves to feed into the sort of unrealistic expectations that Doherty (1996) refers to. This book has illustrated the major flaws in an approach which appears to be myopic insofar as its linear conceptual framework fails to consider the dynamic processes and ideological dissonances, all of which permeate daily work and are mediated by the actors in this real life scenario: the practitioners, the parents, and the children.

The purpose of this research has not been to comment negatively on the quality of child protection work that was visible, though a certain amount of critique has been inevitable. As I moved through the research process from the fieldwork to the analysis and writing up (a trajectory which coincided with my transition from social work into teaching) I began to view the findings more objectively. The combination of a change from my former 'insider' status and the opportunity to review the research data through the theoretical framework, offered me different perspectives on certain aspects of professional practice and enabled me to appreciate, for example, the extent to which the 'liberal compromise' had been adopted by the social workers and the way in which their shared occupational culture operated to influence decision-making. Equally, I had previously considered only the non-statutory practitioners to be guilty of devolving responsibility for the 'dirty work'. Yet the research findings clearly indicate that the statutory social workers too actively contrived to minimise confrontative tasks, albeit in their attempts to make sense of what were sometimes convoluted dilemmas.

At the same time, I am wary of falling into the very trap that this study set out to expose: the presumption of an immutable and easily attained standard against which 'good' and 'bad' practice can be measured. At the heart of this book has been the desire to show that such a hypothesis would be spurious and there is no claim of insight or 'truth' when it comes to measuring the quality of work. Through its methodological paradigm, this study has created rather than proved its findings, by making visible the qualitative issues that necessarily determine processes and outcomes in interventions with children who are the subject of child protection and welfare concerns. The 'official' version tends to be stripped of the contextual and occupational realities of day-to-day work in a way that conceals the very nature of the job. The research on which the book is based has demonstrated that Irish child protection work is far from a static, procedurally governed practice and is, in its current context, not susceptible to such management. It has illustrated the unique way in which a broad range of practitioners in child care work actively shape or manipulate their own discourse in an attempt to address the demands of their professional task. Rather than describing or evaluating child protection work, this book has, by going beyond what is outwardly evident, explored what it 'is', and has attempted to explain why it is. In summary, this challenge to the official orthodoxy of child protection has sought not simply to expose weaknesses in practice and flaws in organisational management, but to make a case for acknowledging the limits and imperfections in a system which relies on such an uncertain and often unrealistic range of human endeavour, and isolates itself from the wider structural factors which perpetuate violence and adversity.

References

Bell, M. (2000) *Child Protection: Families and the Conference Process.* Aldershot: Ashgate.

Blyth, E. and Milner, J. (1990) 'The process of inter-agency work'. In The Violence Against Children Study Group, *Taking Child Abuse Seriously.* London: Routledge.

Buckley, H. (2002) *Child Protection: Innovations and Interventions.* Dublin: Institute of Public Administration.

Buckley, H. (1997) 'Child protection in Ireland'. In M. Harder and K. Pringle (eds) *Protecting Children in Europe: Towards a New Millennium.* Aalborg: University Press.

Buckley, H., Skehill, C. and O'Sullivan, E. (1997) *Child Protection Practices in Ireland: A Case Study.* Dublin: Oak Tree Press.

Buckley, H. (1996) 'Child abuse guidelines in Ireland: For whose protection?' In H. Ferguson and T. McNamara (eds) *Protecting Irish Children: Investigation, Protection and Welfare.* Dublin: Institute of Public Administration.

Bunreacht na hEireann (1937) Constitution of Ireland. Stationery Office.

Butler, S. (1996) 'Child protection or professional self-preservation by the baby nurses? Public health nurses and child protection in Ireland'. *Social Science and Medicine 43*, 303–314.

Cemlyn, S. (2000) 'From neglect to partnership? Challenges for social services in promoting the welfare of traveller children'. In *Child Abuse Review 9*, 349–363.

Cheetham, J., Fuller, R., McIvor, G. and Petch, A. (1992) *Evaluating Social Work Effectiveness.* Buckingham: Open University Press.

Christie, A. (1993) 'Putting carer involvement in child protection conferences into practice'. In H. Ferguson, R. Gilligan and R. Torode (eds) *Surviving Childhood Adversity: Issues for Policy and Practice.* Dublin: Social Studies Press, 190–201.

Claussen, A.H. and Crittenden, P.M. (1991) 'Physical and psychological maltreatment: relations among the types of maltreatment'. *Child Abuse and Neglect 15*, 5.18.

Cleaver, H. and Freeman, P. (1995) *Parental Perspectives in Cases of Suspected Child Abuse.* London: HMSO.

Colwell Report (1974) *Report of the Committee of Inquiry into the Care and Supervision Provided in Relation to Maria Colwell.* London: HMSO.

Corby, B. (1987) *Working with Child Abuse.* Milton Keynes: Open University Press.

Corby, B. (1993) *Child Abuse: Towards a Knowledge Base.* Milton Keynes: Open University Press.

Corby, B. (1995) 'Interprofessional co-operation and interagency co-ordination'. In K. Wilson and A. James (eds) *The Child Protection Handbook.* London: Balliere Tindall.

Corby, B., Millar, M. and Young, L. (1996) 'Parental participation in child protection work: rethinking the rhetoric'. *British Journal of Social Work 26*, 475–492.

Crittenden, P. (1993) 'An information processing perspective on the behaviour of neglectful parents'. *Criminal Justice and Behaviour 20*, 27–48.

Crouch, J. and Milner, J. (1993) 'Effects of child neglect on children'. *Criminal Justice and Behaviour 20*, 49–65.

Daniel, B. and Taylor, J. (2001) *Engaging with Fathers.* London: Jessica Kingsley Publishers.

Denzin, N. (1978) *The Research Act in Sociology: A Theoretical Introduction to Sociological Methods* (2nd edn). New York: McGraw Hill.

Denzin, N. (1994) 'The art and politics of interpretation'. In N. Denzin and Y. Lincoln *Handbook of Qualitative Research.* London: Sage.

Denzin, N. and Lincoln, Y. (1994) 'Entering the field of qualitative research'. *Handbook of Qualitative Research.* London: Sage.

Department of Education (1991) *Procedures for Dealing with Allegations or Suspected Child Abuse.* Dublin: Department of Education.

Department of Health (1976) *Report of the Committee on Non-Accidental Injury to Children.* Dublin: Stationery Office.

Department of Health (1977) *Memorandum on Non-Accidental Injury to Children.* Dublin: Department of Health.

Department of Health (1980) *Guidelines on the Identification and Management of Non-Accidental Injury to Children.* Dublin: Department of Health.

Department of Health (1983) *Guidelines for the Identification, Investigation and Management of Non-Accidental Injury To Children.* Dublin: Department of Health.

Department of Health (1985) *Committee on Social Work Report.* Dublin: Department of Health.

Department of Health (1987) *Child Abuse Guidelines: Guidelines on Procedures for the Identification, Investigation and Management of Child Abuse.* Dublin: Department of Health.

Department of Health (1993) *The Report of the Kilkenny Incest Investigation.* Dublin: Government Publications.

Department of Health (1994) *Shaping a Healthier Future: A Strategy for Effective Healthcare in the 1990s.* Dublin: Stationery Office.

Department of Health (1995) *Notification of Suspected Cases of Child Abuse between Health Boards and Gardaí.* Dublin: Department of Health.

Department of Health (1996a) *Putting Children First: Discussion Document on Mandatory Reporting*. Dublin: Department of Health.

Department of Health (1996b) Child Abuse Statistics.

Department of Health (1997) *Putting Children First: Promoting and Protecting the Rights of Children*. Department of Health.

Department of Health and Children (1999) *Children First: National Guidelines for the Protection and Welfare of Children*. Dublin: Department of Health and Children.

Department of Health and Children (2000) *Preliminary Analysis of Child Care Interim Minimum Data Set 1999*. Dublin: Department of Health.

Department of Health and Children (2002) *Our Duty to Care: Child Protection Guidelines for Community and Voluntary Organisations*. Dublin: Department of Health and Children.

Department of Health and Social Security [UK] (1988) *Protecting Children: A Guide for Social Workers Undertaking a Comprehensive Assessment*. London: HMSO.

Department of Health [UK] (1991) *Working Together – a Guide to Inter-Agency Co-operation for the Protection of Children from Abuse*. London: HMSO.

Department of Health [UK] (1995) *Child Protection: Messages from Research*. London: HMSO.

Department of Health, Home Office, Department for Education and Employment (1999) *Working Together to Safeguard Children*. London: HMSO.

Department of Health, Home Office, Department for Education and Employment (2000) *Framework for the Assessment of Children in Need and Their Families*. London: HMSO.

Dingwall, R., Eekelaar, J. and Murray, T. (1983) *The Protection of Children: State Intervention and Family Life*. Oxford: Blackwell.

Dingwall, R., Eekelaar, J. and Murray, T. (1995, 2nd edn) *The Protection of Children: State Intervention and Family Life*. Oxford: Blackwell.

Dingwall, R. (1980) 'Problems of teamwork in primary care'. In S. Lonsdale, A. Webb and T. Briggs, *Teamwork in the Personal Social Services and Health Care*. London: Croom Helm.

Dingwall, R. (1989) 'Some problems about predicting child abuse and neglect' in O. Stevenson (ed) *Child Abuse: Public Policy and Professional Practice*. Hemel Hempstead: Harvester Wheatsheaf.

Doherty, D. (1996) 'Child care and protection: protecting the children – supporting their service providers'. In H. Ferguson and T. McNamara (eds) *Protecting Irish Children: Investigation, Protection and Welfare*. Dublin: Institute of Public Administration.

Donzelot, J. (1980) *The Policing of Families: Welfare Versus the State*. London: Hutchinson.

Eastern Health Board (1994) *Review of Adequacy of Child Care and Family Support Services in 1994*. Dublin: Eastern Health Board.

Eastern Health Board/Impact Review Group (1997) *Report of the Eastern Health Board/Impact Review Group on Child Care and Family Support Services.* Dublin: Eastern Health Board.

Edwards, J. (1998) 'Screening out men: or "has mum changed her washing powder recently?"' In J. Popay, J. Hearn and J. Edwards (eds) *Men, Gender Divisions and Welfare.* London: Routledge.

Everitt, A. and Hardiker, P. (1996) *Evaluating for Good Practice.* Basingstoke: Macmillan.

Farmer, E. (1993) 'The impact of child protection interventions: the experiences of parents and children'. In L. Waterhouse (ed) *Child Abuse and Child Abusers.* London: Jessica Kingsley Publishers.

Farmer, E. and Owen, M. (1995) *Child Protection Practice: Private Risks and Public Remedies.* London: HMSO.

Farrelly, M., Butler, G. and O'Dalaigh, L. (1993) 'Working with intra-familial child sexual abuse'. In H. Ferguson, R. Gilligan and R. Torode (eds) *Surviving Childhood Adversity: Issues for Policy and Practice.* Dublin: Social Studies Press.

Featherstone, B. (1996) 'Victims or villains? Women who physically abuse their children' In B. Fawcett, B. Featherstone, J. Hearn and C. Toft (eds) *Violence and Gender Relations: Theories and Interventions.* London: Sage.

Featherstone, B. (1997) 'What has gender got to do with it? Exploring physically abusive behaviour towards children'. *British Journal of Social Work 27,* 419–433.

Ferguson, H. (1990) 'Rethinking child protection practices: a case for history'. In The Violence Against Children Study Group, *Taking Child Abuse Seriously.* London: Unwin Hyman.

Ferguson, H. (1991) 'The power to protect abused children: reflections on child protection and the Cleveland affair'. *Irish Social Worker 10,* No.10, pp.7–9.

Ferguson, H. (1993) 'Surviving Irish childhood: child protection and the death of children in child abuse cases in Ireland since 1884'. H. Ferguson, R. Gilligan and R. Torode (eds) *Surviving Childhood Adversity: Issues for Policy and Practice.* Dublin: Social Studies Press.

Ferguson, H. (1994) 'Child abuse inquiries and the Report of the Kilkenny incest investigation: a critical analysis'. *Administration 41,* 385–410.

Ferguson, H. (1995) 'Child welfare, child protection and the Child Care Act 1991: Key issues for policy and practice'. In H. Ferguson and P. Kenny (eds) *On Behalf of the Child: Child Welfare, Child Protection and the Child Care Act 1991.* Dublin: A & A Farmar.

Ferguson, H. (1996) 'Protecting Irish children in time: Child abuse as a social problem and the development of the child protection system in the Republic of Ireland'. In H. Ferguson and T. McNamara (eds) *Protecting Irish Children: Investigation, Protection and Welfare.* Dublin: Institute of Public Administration.

Ferguson, H. (1997) 'Protecting children in new times: Child protection and the risk society'. *Child and Family Social Work 2*, 221–234.

Ferguson, H. and O'Reilly, M. (2001) *Keeping Children Safe: Child Abuse, Child Protection and the Promotion of Welfare.* Dublin: A & A Farmar.

Finkelhor, D. (1994) 'The "Backlash" and the future of child protection advocacy: Insights from the study of social issues'. In J. Myers (ed) *The Backlash: Child Protection Under Fire.* Thousand Oaks: Sage.

Fox Harding, L. (1991, 2nd edn, 1997) *Perspectives in Child Care Policy.* Harlow: Longman.

Gibbons, J. and Bell, C. (1994) 'Variation in operation of English child protection registers'. *British Journal of Social Work 24*, 701–714.

Gibbons, J., Conroy, S. and Bell, C. (1995) *Operating the Child Protection System.* London: HMSO.

Giovannoni, J.M. and Becerra, R.M. (1979) *Defining Child Abuse.* New York: Free Press.

Glaser, D. and Frosh, S. (1988) *Child Sexual Abuse.* London: Macmillan.

Gordon, L. (1989) *Heroes of their own Lives: The Politics and History of Family Violence, Boston 1880-1960.* London: Virago.

Guba, E. and Lincoln, Y. (1994) 'Competing paradigms in qualitative research'. In N. Denzin and Y. Lincoln (eds) *Handbook of Qualitative Research.* Thousand Oaks: Sage.

Hallett, C. and Stevenson, O. (1980) *Child Abuse: Aspects of Interprofessional Co-operation.* London: George Allen & Unwin.

Hallett, C. and Birchall, E. (1992) *Coordination and Child Protection: A Review of the Literature.* Edinburgh: HMSO.

Hallett, C. (1995) *Interagency Coordination in Child Protection.* London: HMSO.

Hill, M. (1997) 'Participatory research with children'. *Child and Family Social Work 2* 171–183.

Hooper, C.A. (1992) *Mothers Surviving Child Sexual Abuse.* London: Routledge.

Horwath, J. (2001) *Child Neglect: Is your View my View?* Ireland: North Eastern Health Board.

Horwath, J. and Morrison, T. (2001) 'Assessment of parental motivation to change'. In J. Horwath (ed) *The Child's World: Assessing Children in Need.* London: Jessica Kingsley Publishers.

Howe, D. (1987) *Introduction to Social Work Theory.* Aldershot: Ashgate.

Howe, D. (1992) 'Child abuse and the bureaucratisation of social work'. *Sociological Review 40*, 490–508.

Howe, D. (1996) 'Surface and depth in social work practice'. In N. Parton (ed) *Social Theory, Social Change and Social Work.* London: Routledge.

Howitt, D. (1992) *Child Abuse Errors.* Hemel Hempstead: Harvester Wheatsheaf.

Hughes, E. (1958) *Men and their Work.* New York: Free Press.

Irish Catholic Bishops' Advisory Committee on Child Sexual Abuse by Priests and Religious (1996) *Child Sexual Abuse: Framework for a Church Response.* Dublin: Veritas.

McCashin, A. (1996) *Lone Mothers in Ireland: A Local Study.* Dublin: Oak Tree Press.

MacDonald, G. (2001) *Effective Interventions for Child Abuse and Neglect.* London: Wiley.

McKeown, K. (2000) *A Guide to What Works in Family Support Services for Vulnerable Families.* Dublin: Government Information Services.

Menzies, I. (1970) *The Functioning of Social Systems as a Defence against Anxiety.* Tavistock Pamphlet No. 3. London: Tavistock Institute of Human Relations.

Milner, J. (1993) 'Avoiding violent men: The gendered nature of child protection policy and practice'. In H. Ferguson, R. Gilligan and R. Torode (eds) *Surviving Childhood Adversity: Issues for Policy and Practice.* Dublin: Social Studies Press.

Milner, J. (1996) 'Men's resistance to social workers'. In B. Fawcett, B. Featherstone, J. Hearn and C. Toft (eds) *Violence and Gender Relations: Theories and Interventions.* London: Sage.

Morrison, T. (1996) 'Partnership and collaboration: Rhetoric and reality'. *Child Abuse and Neglect 20,* 127–140.

Mullender, A. (1996) *Rethinking Domestic Violence: The Social Work and Probation Response.* London: Routledge.

Munro, E. (1996) 'Avoidable and unavoidable mistakes in child protection work'. *British Journal of Social Work 26,* 793–808.

North Western Health Board (1998) *West of Ireland Farmer Case: Report of the Panel of Inquiry.* Manorhamilton: North Western Health Board.

O'Hagan, K. and Dillenberger, K. (1995) *The Abuse of Women within Child Care Work.'* Buckingham: Open University Press.

O'Higgins, K. (1993) 'Surviving separation: Traveller children in substitute care'. H. Ferguson, R. Gilligan and R. Torode (eds) *Surviving Childhood Adversity: Issues for Policy and Practice.* Dublin: Social Studies Press.

Paley (1987) 'Social work and the sociology of knowledge'. *British Journal of Social Work 17,* 169–186.

Parton, C. (1990) 'Women, gender oppression and child abuse'. In The Violence Against Children Study Group, *Taking Child Abuse Seriously.* London: Unwin Hyman.

Parton, N. (1985) *The Politics of Child Abuse.* Basingstoke: Macmillan.

Parton, N. (1990) 'Taking child abuse seriously'. In The Violence Against Children Study Group, *Taking Child Abuse Seriously.* London: Unwin Hyman.

Parton, N. (1991) *Governing the Family: Child Care, Child Protection and the State.* London: Macmillan.

Parton, N. (1996a) 'Child protection, family support, and social work'. *Child and Family Social Work 1,* 3–11.

Parton, N. (1996b) 'Social work, risk and "the blaming system." In N. Parton (ed) *Social Theory, Social Change and Social Work*. London: Routledge.

Parton, N., Thorpe, D. and Wattam, C. (1997) *Child Protection, Risk and the Moral Order*. London: Macmillan.

Parton, N. (1997) 'Child protection and family support: Current debates and future prospects'. In N. Parton (ed) *Child Protection and Family Support: Tensions, Contradictions and Possibilities*. London: Routledge.

Parton, N. and O'Byrne, P. (2000) *Constructive Social Work: Towards a New Practice*. Basingstoke: Macmillan.

Parton, N. and Mathews, R. (2001) 'New directions in child protection and family support in Western Australia: a policy initiative to re-focus child welfare practice.' *Child and Family Social Work 6*, 97–113.

Pithouse, A. (1987) *Social Work: The Social Organisation of an Invisible Trade*. Aldershot: Gower.

Polnay, J. (2000) 'General practitioners and child protection case conference participation: Reasons for non-attendance and proposals for a way forward'. *Child Abuse Review 9*, 108–123.

Powell, F. (1997) 'Social work, postmodernity and civil society'. In *Administration 45*, 61–71.

Prochaska, J. and Di Clementi, C. (1982) 'Transtheoretical therapy: towards a more integrative model of change'. *Psychotherapy Theory, Research and Practice, 19(3)*.

Reder, P., Duncan, S. and Gray, M. (1993) *Beyond Blame: Child Abuse Tragedies Revisited*. London: Routledge.

Reder, P. and Duncan, S. (1998) *Lost Innocents: A Follow-up Study of Fatal Child Abuse*. London: Routledge.

Rodger, J. (1996) *Family Life and Social Control: A Sociological Perspective*. Basingstoke, Macmillan.

Ryan, M. (2000) *Working with Fathers*. London: HMSO.

Scott, D. (1997) 'Inter-agency conflict: an ethnographic study'. *Child and Family Social Work 2*, 73–80.

Sharland, E., Seal, H., Croucher, M., Aldgate, J. and Jones, D. (1996) *Professional Intervention in Child Sexual Abuse*. London: HMSO.

Smith, G. and Cantley, C. (1985) *Assessing Health Care: A Study in Organisational Evaluation*. Milton Keynes: University Press.

Stevenson, O. (1989) *Public Policy and Professional Practice*. London: Harvester Wheatsheaf.

Stevenson, O. (1995) 'Case conferences in child protection'. In K. Wilson and A. James (eds) *The Child Protection Handbook*. Balliere Tindall, 227–241.

Stevenson, O. (1996) 'Emotional abuse and neglect: a time for reappraisal'. *Child and Family Social Work 1*, 13–18.

Stevenson, O. (1997) 'Child welfare in the UK: the exercise of professional judgements by social workers'. Paper presented to the BASPCAN Congress, July 1997, Edinburgh.

Stevenson, O. (1998) *Child Neglect: Issues and Dilemmas.* London: Blackwell.

Stevenson, O. (1999) (ed) *Child Welfare in the UK.* London: Blackwell.

Task Force on the Travelling Community (1995) *Report of the Task Force on the Travelling Community.* Dublin: Government Publications.

Thoburn, J. (1993) 'Some issues of decision-making in child protection'. In H. Ferguson, R. Gilligan and R. Torode (eds) *Surviving Childhood Adversity: Issues for Policy and Practice.* Dublin: Social Studies Press.

Thoburn, J., Lewis, A. and Shemmings, D. (1995) *Paternalism or Partnership? Family Involvement in the Child Protection Process.* London: HMSO.

Thorpe, D. (1994) *Evaluating Child Protection.* Milton Keynes: Open University Press.

Thorpe, D. (1997) 'Regulating late modern childrearing in Ireland'. *Economic and Social Review 28,* 63–84.

Torode, R., Walsh, T. and Woods, M. (2001) *Working with Refugees and Asylum Seekers: A Social Work Resource Book.* Dublin: Department of Social Studies, Trinity College.

Trinder, L. (1996) 'Social work research: the state of the art (or science)'. *Child and Family Social Work 1,* 233–242.

Tunstill, J. and Aldgate J. (2000) *Services for Children in Need.* London: HMSO.

Wattam, C. (1997) 'Is the criminalisation of child harm and injury in the interests of the child?' *Children and Society 11,* 97–107.

Western Health Board (1996) *Kelly – A Child is Dead.* Interim Report of the Joint Committee on the Family, Dublin. Government Publications Office.

Whittington, C. (1983) 'Social work in the welfare network'. *British Journal of Social Work 13,* 265–86.

Wise, S. (1989) *Child Abuse Procedures and Social Work Practice: An Ethnographic Approach.* Ph.D Book: University of Manchester.

Wise, S. (1990) 'Becoming a feminist social worker'. In L. Stanley (ed) *Feminist Praxis: Research, Theory and Epistemology in Feminist Sociology.* London: Routledge.

Wise, S. (1995) 'Feminist ethics in practice'. In R. Hugman and D. Smith (eds) *Ethical Issues in Social Work.* London: Routledge.

Yin, R. (1994) *Case Study Research: Design and Methods.* Newbury Park and London: Sage.

Subject Index

Author Index

'THE BEAST'
DIEGO COSTA

CHRIS DAVIES

JB

JOHN BLAKE

First published by
John Blake Publishing Limited
3 Bramber Court, 2 Bramber Road
London W14 9PB

www.johnblakepublishing.co.uk

www.facebook.com/johnblakebooks ⬛
twitter.com/jblakebooks ⬛

First published in paperback in 2015

ISBN: 978-1-78418-650-0

The right of Chris Davies to be identified as the author of this work
has been asserted by him in accordance with the Copyright,
Designs and Patents Act 1988.

Papers used by John Blake Publishing are natural, recyclable products made
from wood grown in sustainable forests. The manufacturing processes
conform to the environmental regulations of the country of origin.

Every attempt has been made to contact the relevant copyright-holders,
but some were unobtainable. We would be grateful if the
appropriate people could contact us.